OTHER EARTHS

ALIEN LIFE

NASA's Kepler Mission...
Prepare Yourself with a Christian Spaceview

Kenneth Paul Dykstra, M.A.

www.ChristianSpaceview.com

Join the conversation on Facebook:
Other Earths/Alien Life: A Christian Spaceview

Other Earths / Alien Life:
NASA's Kepler Mission…
Prepare Yourself with a Christian Spaceview

Cover design by Jennifer Hines

Second Edition
Redemption Tree Press
Copyright ©2013 / Kenneth Paul Dykstra

All rights reserved.
ISBN: 978-0-578-12359-2

This work is licensed. To view a copy of this license, visit http://creativecommons.org/licenses/by-nc/2.5 or visit http://www.lulu.com.

TABLE OF CONTENTS

ABOUT THE AUTHOR	VII
PART I - OTHER EARTHS	**VIII**
PROLOGUE	1
1. KEPLER MISSION	7
2. HABITABLE WORLDS	21
3. THE ROAD TO THIS PIVOTAL MOMENT	33
PART II - ALIEN LIFE	**46**
4. WHERE THE ROAD LEADS NEXT	47
5. ARE WE ALONE?	68
6. ALIEN LIFE	81
7. INTELLIGENT ALIEN LIFE	99
8. WOULD THEY KNOW JESUS?	113
PART III - A CHRISTIAN SPACEVIEW	**119**
9. FAITH: A CHRISTIAN SPACEVIEW	120
10. TIME: A CHRISTIAN SPACEVIEW	135
11. END-TIMES QUAGMIRE	149
12. WE'VE LISTENED…WATCHED…	157
EPILOGUE	169
REFERENCES	171

PREFACE

- Unless otherwise noted, all scripture references are from THE HOLY BIBLE: NEW INTERNATIONAL VERSION®. NIV®. Copyright© 1973, 1978, 1984 by Biblica. All rights reserved worldwide.

- THE HOLY BIBLE: NEW LIVING TRANSLATION. NLT®. Copyright© 1996, 2004 by Tyndale Charitable Trust. All rights reserved.

- When explaining how to locate stars or constellations, my perspective is from a 42 degree north latitude (Grand Rapids, MI).

- I use the term "scientist" to include physicists, mathematicians, and professional astronomers. I use the terms "physics" and "math" to include all forms of physics from the highly theoretical to the applied. I use the term "religion" or "religious" to entail all major world religions in the broadest sense.

- I also present my writing with St. Augustine's short human timeline in mind as opposed to the billions of years modern science theorizes. In Augustine's famous work, *City Of God*, he reasons that the impressive rate human civilization has progressed indicates a short human history. Stephen Hawking acknowledges this argument in his latest book.[1]

- Throughout this book, I refer to God in the male gender, "He," for the sole purpose of communicating the relational, personal aspects of God. Scripture clearly reveals that God is Spirit

---

[1] Hawking, Stephen & Mlodinow L. *The Grand Design*. Bantam Books: New York, 2010. Print. (p.124)

(John 4:24) and not a "He" or a "She." This is critical to remember when thinking of God. Associating God with human attributes, though potentially dangerous, is needed and known theologically as "anthropomorphism." The purpose of projecting human characteristics onto God is to help our finite minds relate to an eternal Triune God. Atheists like Stephen Hawking and Richard Dawkins point out this anthropomorphic exercise as proof that God is merely made up by the desperate minds of men. This is a weak argument.

- I do not mean to promote the Platonic/Greek origins of the term "soul" but only use it since readers readily understand this term in general. Immaterial/spiritual would be more accurate and I use them interchangeably.

- The term "god-less" was chosen over "godless" since "god-less" emphasizes people that live life less God; whereas the term "godless" tends to carry an evil sense to it, which is a stigma I want to avoid.

- Entropy is not evil but only evidence of a broken Creation caused by Sin.

- And finally, one will notice a tension within this work between faith and science. When each discipline is critically considered, devaluing neither, tension is found and this is part of the wonder and mystery of life.

Dominion and awe belong to God;
He establishes order in the heights of heaven.

—*Job 25:2*

ABOUT THE AUTHOR

Kenneth Paul Dykstra accomplished a Master of Arts in Systematic Theology from Grand Rapids Theological Seminary and a Bachelor of Science in World Religions from Western Michigan University. He has served as a deacon, elder, traveling pastor, and jail preacher.

His hobbies include 25 years in amateur astronomy, touring historic observatories and a world-renowned optics company between business trips. Ken marvels at the new technology and breath-taking discoveries during this second golden age of astronomy; it has once again changed the way the world thinks of the heavens.

He is married to Crisi, his beautiful bride of twenty years and together chase two beautiful kids, Chelsea and Justin. Ken has traveled North America speaking and teaching for two manufacturing companies. Carving out time between work, ministry and kids; he integrates his knowledge of scripture and theology with his life-long hobby, astronomy…a field rarely written on in the Christian community. Ken and his family reside in the greater Grand Rapids, MI community.

For the latest information on NASA's Kepler Mission, go to: **www.christianspaceview.com**.

PART I
OTHER EARTHS

*Earth is the cradle of humanity,
but one cannot remain in the cradle forever.*

~Kanstantin E. Tsiolkovsky

PROLOGUE

*Astronomy compels the soul to look
upward and leads us from this world to another.*

~Plato
342 B.C.

Cloaked in darkness, I listen to the chorus of crickets playing their timeless symphony, no lights, no cars, no humans—perfect. A smirk creeps across my face, *A little me time.* I say to myself. Feeling around the trunk of my car, I find the three gray cases as my eyes adjust to midnight. With anticipation mounting, my thoughts betray me once again in a whisper, *No responsibilities...at least for a little while.* The shape of the cases slowly appear out of the blackness as my eyes adjust to night vision. Opening them, ancient light from countless stars traveling millions of miles and thousands of years finally discover their purpose, reflecting off my beloved telescope to help me see. And this childhood love still brings a smile to my face. Gazing upon my telescope takes me back and fills my heart with deep appreciation, *Thank you God.* swells up from within me. Gingerly lifting them out of thick gray padding, I saddle the telescope tube to the mount my father made for me and place them both on a wood tripod. Without looking, I brush my fingers over the rack of eyepieces: 4mm…12.5mm…25mm… and like a child just home from trick-or-treating, I quickly consider which one to pick, selecting my favorite one every time—the 12.5mm. This eyepiece always proves the grandest, crispest view of what awaits me. Slewing the scope, I align it to a location in the night sky I know by heart, and there in the cross-hairs of my finder-scope lies the prize.

Squinting to catch the show playing inside, I am dazzled with four hundred billion stars swirling into a majestic single glow, Andromeda Galaxy. Light waves from our closest neighbor galaxy have been traveling since before Stonehenge was even thought of, ancient light crossing the ocean of deep space from an alien place only to finish their journey in my eye. *It's real.* I whisper, just to hear me proclaim it. *It's really out there.* Confessing again, as if to convince myself. And as I study it, the wonderment turns to puzzlement, stirring the same questions I asked myself the first time I captured its light in my scope as a boy: *Why God...why create this beautiful swirling masterpiece, and so far away, is it just a tease?* And yet these questions never grow old: *Does that galaxy with all those stars harbor planets like ours...does it hold life? Why doesn't the Bible say anything about such places? And why make a vast universe with so much in it if we are all there is?* Each glance into my favorite eyepiece with each star cluster and galaxy that I view begs for answers. They exist before our very eyes every night and have a spectacular story to share. And I wonder, once again, who the story is for...is it for us? Is it for God? Or is it for others?

Delve with me into these questions. Learn of a new space race now obsessing astronomers around the world and how it plays a key role in these ageless questions. See how NASA's Kepler Spacecraft is spear-heading this new race and learn of its mission goals that will prove historical in their findings. And most importantly, explore the questions of faith Kepler's mission beckons. May King David's words, *Blessed is the man who finds wisdom, the man who gains understanding (Proverbs 3:13),* resonate within your soul as you read and learn in these pages about an Ancient Testament predating the Old Testament. Allow the immensity of space and time to overwhelm you while learning of a reality cradling our planet that extends far beyond us and our solar system and even our Milky Way galaxy. A cosmos that is vastly greater than our Local Cluster of galaxies and beyond our Super Cluster of countless galaxies, which our galaxy disappears into. And all this is still just a cul-de-sac in God's sprawling, ever expanding Creation. And in this humble state, rediscover timeless truth in an ancient faith. Truths older than all you can see at night—after your eyes have adjusted, not to night vision, but to God's vision and a Christian Spaceview.

Countdown Begins

To begin then, let's back up to where the countdown for NASA's launch of the Kepler Spacecraft truly began...three thousand years ago...when light waves from one hundred and fifty six thousand stars began their epic race to Earth. Streaking across the heavens at a blinding speed that even time cannot catch, these light waves and the information they contain have remained unchanged—unlike human civilizations...

Three thousand years ago, 1000 B.C. on Earth. Greece ushers in a whole new age for humans by refining a lighter, stronger armament made of Iron. Their enemies' very best shields of bronze are no match, and the blood of western culture is born in this new Iron Age. While in the East, Asia Minor comes to the fore with the Phoenicians developing the first non-pictorial alphabet that is the forerunner to Latin, making hieroglyphs obsolete. In Egypt, the mighty dynasty of Ramesses[2] has ended and a country is in chaos while Israel's shepherd boy killed Palestine's champion and later as commander, captured the city of Jebus renaming it Jerusalem.[3] On the other side of the

---

[2] Dunn, James. *Ramesses XI: The Last New Kingdom Pharaoh.* n.d. Web. 26 Mar. 2010.
<http://touregypt.net/featurestories/ramessesxi.htm>

planet, a vast land exists but is only known to cannibals having just settled there in what we now call the Yucatan peninsula of Mexico. And light from 156,000 stars located in the Northern Cross begins its journey toward an unseen destination: Earth.

One thousand years later, that same light is still silently streaking by, it is now 0 A.D. The glory of the Iron Age is in full swing with the Greco-Roman Empire at its zenith conquering lands from Israel to Briton.[4] In the East, the Han Dynasty, under the cunning leadership of Qin Shi Huang, pushes back the Mongolian menace and builds a Great Wall to keep them out. Now, a unified China enjoys peace and high culture that they have never matched again, developing Confucius philosophy[5] and amassing riches from a treacherous road to a western land obsessed with their silk. Foreseeing his own death, Emperor Huang immortalizes himself with the commissioning of the still intact Terra-Cotta Army surrounding his tomb with Huang himself shown leading the charge of 130 stone chariots, 520 stone horses, and 8,000 stone soldiers, meticulously crafted and still guarding him.[6] Astrologers from his dynasty and two of its neighbors, inform their kings of a remarkable appearance in the night sky of a new star. These three countries send entourages, most likely armed, along the dangerous Silk Road to the West in search of this prophesied baby-King. The stage is now set in Bethlehem for the establishment of a new religion, unlike any faith ever attempted. While light from 156,000 stars located in the area of the Northern Cross continues its one thousand year old journey...

---

[3] 1 Chronicles 11:4
[4] Today's Great Britain.
[5] Man, John. *The Terra Cotta Army*. Da Capo Press, 2008. Print.
[6] Ibid, p.2

Two thousand years later, light from those same ancient stars continue their long sojourn toward Earth, it is now 1000 A.D. The collapse of the mighty Roman Empire is a distant memory from five centuries past leaving only ruins of great coliseums and temples. The barbaric Visigoths who laid siege to Rome and plundered it have also disappeared from the world map without a trace. Meanwhile, Muslim aggression against Christians have reached a boiling point with the takeover of the Holy Sepulcher,[7] the proclaimed burial site of Jesus Christ, causing Pope Urban II to finally call the Church to arms. Eight crusades lasting three centuries take back only a fraction of the sites and churches symbolizing the roots of western architecture and culture dating back to the first Basilica built by Constantine the Great, one of Rome's last great emperors.[8] And during these wars, a supernova flashes and burns for days in the night sky visible to the naked eye as recorded by Chinese and Arab historians; today, we can now observe the remains of that nuclear holocaust known as the Crab Nebula (M1) in the constellation Taurus. And also during this time, the Viking, Leif Ericson,[9] voyages out across the icy North Atlantic discovering Iceland, Greenland, and Vinland.[10] But this

---

[7] The Holy Sepulcher is recognized as the burial site of Jesus Christ by historians and Church tradition.

[8] In this century (1096 A.D.) the first Crusade is launched from Rome and heavily aided by the Byzantine Empire, which used to be the old Western Roman Empire. There were eight crusades in all, ending in 1291A.D.

[9] Several famous accounts of his journey confirm this as well as the Catholic Church who nicknamed him the "Evangelizing Explorer". He came to Christ under King Olaf 1 of Norway. For more information: Jackson, Ed. "Statue in Reykjavik, Iceland of the discoverer of the North American Continent." University of Alberta (Canada), n.d.; Lynn, Ryne, *Leif Ericson, Columbus' Predecessor by Nearly 500 Years.*, n.d. Web. 26 Mar. 2010

[10] Today's New Foundland.

new world, Vinland, is still five hundred years away from the eyes of Christopher Columbus[11] and hiding a savage secret. Approaching their bloody zenith, the Mayans sacrifice men, women, children, and babies, some of whom they eat to honor their gods. While light from 156,000 stars continues its two thousand year old relentless journey toward an unseen destination…Earth.

It is now 2009 A.D., three thousand years into their journey: *3…2…1…we have liftoff of the Kepler Spacecraft, God speed.* It is the evening of March 6, Cape Canaveral Air Force Station, NASA. A new breed of scope has just been launched. It isn't looking for the edge of the universe or black holes or galaxies; the prize in mind is impossibly small and produces no light of its own. Kepler is the first[12] telescope solely designed to dissect light waves in search of a very special class of planet. Its sole mission is to study one hundred and fifty six thousand hand-picked stars in the Northern Cross to locate worlds similar to our Earth in every way: same temperature, size, gravity, and climate. Kepler is now hunting Earths. And ancient light from 156,000 stars launched from the Northern Cross, has finally been captured by a precision instrument fashioned from the hands of modern men and women. The news NASA has for us on what Kepler discovers will change the way our world looks out at the heavens.

We are on the brink of something wonderful, I fear.

---

[11] 1492 A.D.
[12] The French Space Agency in corroboration with the European Space Agency launched COROT (COnvection ROtation and planetary Transits) to search the heavens for planets but it did not have the resolving power of Kepler. It failed to identify planets Earth size or smaller and failed to identify planets in habitable zones.

1. KEPLER MISSION

All truths are easy to understand once they are discovered; the point is to discover them.

~Galileo Galilei
(1564–1642)

USA Today[13] plasters a large image of the night-time launch from Cape Canaveral declaring: "Kepler's On a Mission to Discover Earths."[14] The next day *Fox News* highlights the spectacular night-time liftoff and five months later, *The Diane Rehm Show* interviews part of the Kepler science team on *National Public Radio* (NPR) titled, "The Search for Extraterrestrial Life."[15] Across the Atlantic, the BBC also reports the latest updates on NASA's search for other Earths.[16] Every year since the launch, TV, Radio and internet sites air programs with titles like, "Alien Earths" highlighting the Kepler Mission.[17] As you can see by national and international media attention, the anticipation of what this mission is discovering runs high. It receives as much or more news coverage than any other spacecraft,

---

[13] March 5, 2009
[14] Vergano, Dan. "Kepler's on a mission to discover 'Earths.'" *USA Today,* 5 Mar. 2009, Section 6D. Print.
[15] "The Search for Extraterrestrial Life." Narr. Diane Rehm. *The Diane Rehm Show*. Natl. Public Radio. WAMU, Washington, 20 Aug. 2009. Radio. Kepler Science Team attendees: Jill Tarter, Jon Jenkins, Alan Boss.
[16] Narr. Pamela Rutherford. *World Today*. BBC on National Public Radio WUOM, Ann Arbor, Michigan. 11 Sept. 2010. Radio.
[17] "Alien Earths," NGEO, Charter Communications, Grand Rapids. 15 Aug. 2010. Schedule available online at: <http://channel.nationalgeographic.com/tv-schedule> Web, 19 Aug. 2010.

with the only exception being the politically-correct International Space Station. Discussions on habitable worlds and alien life are taken seriously, to the tune of $600 million for the Kepler Mission alone. Ball Aerospace, Ames Research Center and Jet Propulsion Laboratory spent fourteen years designing and fabricating the hardware and software for this quest. A mission that may prove as historical as Christopher Columbus' discovery of the new world in 1492 or Nicolas Copernicus' book, *On the Revolutions of the Celestial Spheres.*[18] His book demythologized the conceit that Earth was the center of the universe. Those with a genuine faith in God's Word received his shocking news with a broad range of emotions from great praise to great anger, and as I talk to people about Kepler's mission to discover other Earths, my experiences have confirmed the same spectrum of emotions.

First, let's review this exciting and ambitious mission. We'll dissect the technology employed in the spacecraft and what this mission has discovered so far. We'll also delve into the controversial character this mission is named after and why his body is being exhumed from the grave yet again. His life, you will find, is a movie producer's dream. With the mission and its technology understood, we will then launch into key discoveries in classical and quantum physics to aid our discussion. Christian theology does not need science, but I believe science carried out correctly, confirms the fingerprints of God in His Creation. From here, we will explore the deep questions that come from pondering the idea of other Earths and alien life. I believe your heart will be encouraged and faith strengthened. I also believe you will

---

[18] Actually, it was written in Latin: *De Revolutionibus Orbium Coelestium.*

enjoy a new found confidence in recognizing scientific fact from scientific mis-interpretation that is clouding this mission today. Let's prepare ourselves with a Christian Spaceview.

Kepler Spacecraft

The spacecraft measures fifteen feet in length and nine feet in diameter, weighing in at 2,320 pounds. It saw "first light"[19] on April 8, 2009 and is now careening through space in an Earth-trailing orbit around the sun at 66,615 mph (18 miles per second).[20] Kepler gathers light with a 55 inch diameter primary mirror, making it only about half the size of the Hubble Space Telescope's 94.5 inch main mirror.

Kepler uses a corrector lens in front known as a "Schmidt Corrector" for a much wider field of view; Hubble does not. To give you an idea of just how many stars Kepler can see at the same time, when it gets dark tonight, go outside and hold one of your hands in front of you at arm's length. Spread out all five fingers and refocus your eyes on the night sky behind them. This is pretty close to the area Kepler is covering all at once. In technical terms, it is about 105 degrees wide by 105 degrees high, whereas a typical amateur astronomer's telescope can see only about 1 degree wide by 1 degree high. Once this ancient starlight enters the front of the telescope, it immediately passes through a corrector lens in front that slightly spreads the light waves out, so to speak, as it travels back to the primary mirror. The primary mirror then highly concentrates the light back up the tube to its

---

[19] Astronomers term for when a telescope is used for the first time to view the heavens.
[20] A region in Cygnus along the Orion Arm centered on galactic coordinate (76.32°,+13.5°) or RA: 19h 22m 40s, Dec: +44° 30' 00' .

final destination. After travelling three thousand years, this ancient starlight is finally captured by technology crafted from human hands. The technology includes a super-sized photometer packed with forty-two CCD[21] imagers to absorb these timeless waves of information. A CCD imager is what your digital camera uses to absorb light, digitize it, and then re-display it on a screen for you to see. The CCD in your camera, however, is only about the size of your thumbnail, whereas each CCD imager in Kepler is almost 10 times that size.[22]

While receiving a personal tour of Meade Instruments™ in southern California, I was able to watch the polishing and coating process of the optics for the Schmidt-Newtonian style telescopes, which is the same style Kepler employs. Kepler's lens and mirror, however, is not manufactured to produce a crisp, sharp finely focused image as the ones being finely polished at Meade Instruments, but instead, Bell Aerospace engineered the image to be defocused, blurry.[23] To understand why, tonight, go outside and look up at the stars and choose a bright star to stare at. While remaining focused on that star, become aware of the dim stars you see around it with your peripheral vision. While still staring at that bright star, in your mind select the dimmest one in your periphery, and then look directly at it, what happens? It disappears. You can't see it when you try to focus right on it. The defocused light in our peripheral vision causes it to appear bigger than

---

[21] CCD is an abbreviation for 'charge-coupled device.'
[22] Kepler's CCD's are 2 inches long by 1 inch wide with a whopping 2200 x 1024 pixels each.
[23] It is defocused by 10 arcseconds, which is 1/360 of a degree. An arcsecond is 1/60 of an arcminute, which is 1/60 of a degree. There are 360 degrees in a circle. So an arcsecond is 1/3600 of a degree. As it pertains to astronomy, if you stand outside at night looking at the stars and fully extend your arm with your thumb up (like the Fonz) your thumb covers about 2 degrees of sky.

it really is, providing a greater area of light for us to see it with. When you try to focus right on it, your eye seems to make it smaller causing the already dim object to fade out, to seem to disappear. No matter how hard you blink and stare and try to focus on what you know is there, you won't see it. Just like our peripheral vision, Kepler is designed to create the same basic effect. It will need every bit of this capability to recognize the subtle shifts in star brightness that transiting planets cause.

Northern Cross

Of all the regions of space NASA could choose Kepler to study, they chose the Northern Cross.[24]

They chose the Northern Cross because it is well known among astronomers for its concentration of main-sequence stars like our Sun. Astronomers have learned from studying our galaxy and other galaxies that new stars, main-sequence stars, and old-dying stars, tend to "hang out" in their own regions. These regions can be identified by the overall color of the stars in that region. For example, when you look at an image of a galaxy and see a region that has an overall light pink or bright blue hue to it, this tends to be due to all the new-born stars in that specific region, while a region prominent with main-sequence stars shows more blue-white and yellow hues, whereas old and dying star regions glow orange-red. The center of most galaxies glow orange-red while their central spiral arms tend to glow blue-white and yellow, and the outermost regions look pink and bright blue. Our Northern Cross is in one of the central arms of our galaxy. Unlike new stars and old

---

[24] The Northern Cross is not a constellation but known as an Asterism, which is a popular known shape within a constellation, in this case, the constellation Cygnus. The Big Dipper is another popular asterism within the constellation Ursa Major.

stars, a main sequence star is a star that has matured and entered a stable cycle of nuclear fusion, like our Sun.

I find great joy in looking up at the Northern Cross. Its grandeur in the heavens reminds me of God's providence. To find the Northern Cross, on a clear summer night, look exactly straight up and you'll see a bright prominent star named Vega looking straight down back at you. Now look just to the East of Vega at the next brightest star you see; this is Deneb, the star at the top of the Northern Cross. Smack-dab between these two bright stars is where Kepler hunts for other Earths. The stars in this viewing area are part of the center arm in our galaxy known as the Orion Arm. And fortunately, this arm has a peninsula jutting out and away from all the dust and debris within the central plane of our galaxy. Astronomers call this peninsula the Orion Spur. And where do you think God placed our solar system?

That's right, sticking out of that spur. We have the best seats in the house. From these box seats we can enjoy a rare event that plays out only a few weeks each year from mid-July to mid-August. It is at this juncture we can see an unhindered view of both the inner spiral arm, thru the constellation Sagittarius, and the outer spiral arm, through the constellation Perseus. Wait until midnight during the "dog days" of summer and face south. Gaze just above the trees and you are looking toward the constellation Sagittarius and the inner arm. Now turn around to the Northeast and look up high to find the constellation Perseus and the outer arm. All these stars you see are in our spectacular four hundred billion star galaxy.[25]

---

[25] Some scientist estimate the Milky Way is comprised of as many as 500 billion stars (500,000,000,000). Twenty years ago, scientist thought the Milky Way only had 100 billion stars. This is a good illustration of how much room for error science allows themselves when it comes to

Kepler does not see all these stars, of course, it sees about four and half million stars in the Northern Cross sliver of space. Out of these stars, it is programmed to only study the light of about a hundred and fifty thousand main-sequence stars. This sliver accounts for only about .000025% of the stars in our galaxy.[26] The light from the furthest of these special stars is over three thousand light years from us. This means the light we now see may have begun its sojourn when King David just took the throne, before the Silk Road connecting the West to the Far East was known, and even before the beautiful Crab Nebula exploded into existence.[27] But this ancient starlight is not Kepler's ultimate goal. From this starlight, NASA calculates over twelve hundred of them contain a unique light-wave signature. [28] These special stars will show a faint rhythmic dip in brightness, and upon closer review with ground-based telescopes, the stars producing this dip in brightness actually wobble.[29] Stars viewed from outer-space, outside the ever-changing turbulent canopy of our atmosphere, should not wink and wobble. Their light should remain steady and still...at least, that used to be the thinking.

---

the study of the universe. Also, there are a few stars seen by the naked eye that are actually other galaxies, but very few.

[26] For details go to www.kepler.nasa.gov.

[27] It would have been amazing to see in broad daylight a star appear in the blue sky and remain for several days then fade away as recorded by Chinese and Arab Astronomers in 1054 A.D. The Crab Nebulae is now viewable through most telescopes—the remnants from the spectacular supernova explosion.

[28] "The Search for Extraterrestrial Life." Narr. Diane Rehm. *The Diane Rehm Show*. National Public Radio. WAMU, Washington, 20 Aug. 2010. Radio. Kepler Science Team attendees: Jill Tarter, Jon Jenkins, Alan Boss.

[29] I will not be discussing the third method established by Einstein's Gravitational Lansing whereby the planet goes behind the star causing it to momentarily brighten.

51 Pegasi

That all changed in 1995 when Michel Mayor and Didier Queloz published their discovery of the first planet orbiting a main sequence star named 51 Pegasi, fifty light years away.[30] To give you an idea of distance, if you could cruise at the speed of light, 186,000 miles per second, it would take fifty years to get there. Currently, our spacecrafts are nowhere close to such speeds. The Kepler Spacecraft would take around seventy thousand years to get to this star, which is one of our closer neighbors.

To look at 51 Pegasi in the night sky, wait for Fall and face the southern horizon and look up about half-way, which is about forty-five degrees. You will find a great big square made up of four prominent stars that are the most well-known part of the constellation Pegasus, and aptly named, "The Great Square." On the right-hand side of the square and midway up, on a very clear and dark night, you might be able to see 51 Pegasi with the naked eye, a small dim light only 5.5 in magnitude. This anti-climactic star shows a wobble and rhythmic dip in brightness when measured with precision instruments. Mayor and Queloz confirmed that an object orbiting this star is tugging on it. Further studies by other ground based telescopes ruled out all possibilities to explain this star's odd behavior, except one.[31] The very first planet around another star was discovered.

---

[30] Powell, Corey. "Unlikely Places." *Scientific American 266*, March 1992: 22. Print. To be technically accurate, in 1992, Alexander Wolszczan identified an exoplanet but it isn't orbiting an active star; but a dead star known as a pulsar (a star that went Supernova long ago).
[31] Possible causes are Binary stars, which are two stars orbiting each other, or Brown Dwarf stars. Brown Dwarfs are "wannabes" but too small to reach critical mass for nuclear fusion. Nuclear fusion is the engine of a star.

Bellerophon

And on that day a new space race was launched. With the discovery of a world designated "51 Pegasi b" being the reason for these wobbles and dips, a new word was formed: *exoplanets*. Along with this word came a new frontier for astronomers around the world: planet hunting. And most profound is the challenge of a new perspective for humans to grasp—no longer do we just see pinpoints of light when we look up at the stars, but possible Suns of other Earths.

The nickname given to this exoplanet is Bellerophon, which is the name of the mythological Greek hero who captured the famous winged-horse Pegasus. To describe what Bellerophon generally looks like, have you ever looked at Jupiter in the night sky? It's very easy to find on any clear night of the year with your naked eye. It is one of the brightest "stars" in the night sky. Like Jupiter, this newly discovered planet is also a behemoth gas planet; but unlike Jupiter's twelve year orbit, this exoplanet only takes about four Earth days to complete one orbit around its star. Its orbit is so tight, astrophysicists calculate it to be tidally locked, meaning that the planet always shows the same side to its star. Our Moon is also tidally locked to Earth, we never see the dark side of the moon.[32] Because of this, it is calculated that Bellerophon's temperature is approximately eighteen hundred degrees Fahrenheit on the daylight side. Aluminum, for example, melts into molten liquid at twelve hundred degrees Fahrenheit. Although this super-heated Jupiter-size planet is far from being another Earth, its discovery causes one to wonder: Are there other Earths out there?

---

[32] There actually is no dark side to the Moon. We never see the other side of the Moon but as the Moon orbits Earth and Earth the Sun, the Sun does indeed shine on all sides of the Moon.

Let's study the science of wobbles and dips, known as Spectral Analysis, to find out how NASA's Kepler Spacecraft and science teams are on the very brink of answering this age-old question.

Spectral Analysis

Although Kepler's hardware is of the very latest technology, the science is old. Spectral Analysis[33] arguably began in Sir Isaac Newton's chambers in 1666 when he studied the rainbow made from sunlight. Presenting his findings to the Royal Society six years later, he writes,

> *I procured me a Triangular glass-Prisme, to try therewith the celebrated Phenomena of Colours. And in order having darkened my chamber, and made a small hole in my window-shuts, to let in a convenient quantity of the Suns light, I placed my Prisme at this entrance, that it might thereby be refracted to the opposite wall...Comparing the length of this coloured spectrum with its breadth, I found it about five times greater; a disproportion so extravagant, that it excited me to a more than ordinary curiosity of examining, from whence it might proceed.*[34]

Over one hundred and forty years would pass from these rudimentary beginnings before an international race to master Spectral Analysis was sparked across Europe to America in the 1800s. The new discipline was at full-speed

---

[33] Spectral Analysis is a facet of spectroscopy used by astronomers.
[34] Hearnshaw, J.B. *The Analysis of Starlight: One Hundred and Fifty Years of Astronomical Spectroscopy*. Cambridge University Press Syndicate: New York, 1986. Print. (p.20)

with such well-known names as John Herschel, Joseph Fraunhoffer, and many others forging the way. On the shoulders of these pioneers comes Gustav Kirchhoff and Robert Bunsen (yes, of the famous Bunsen burner used in all chemistry labs around the world today). These men ushered in modern Spectral Analysis so critical to Kepler's hunt for other Earths today.[35] They honed the skill of reading light, showing it as an ideal information carrier since it does not rust, corrode, or wear out.

A rainbow is Spectral Analysis on display for all mankind to enjoy. When sunlight passes through a raindrop, the light is bent due to the non-uniform shape of the raindrop acting like a prism, creating a rainbow. Genesis 2:5–6 declares rain did not yet exist and reveals a glimpse of how the Earth was watered before rain. The rebellious human race had never seen rain, meaning they had never seen a rainbow. Genesis 7 is when rain is mentioned for the first time. The Bible records how God commanded Noah to build an Ark due to the deluge of rain to come. After the Forty days of rain, the Bible records how Spectral Analysis forever became a symbol of God's anger to be revered, His mercy to be recognized, and His promise to never allow such a flood again—the rainbow.

Types Of Spectrum

There are three types of rainbows that scientists call spectrums: Continuous Spectrum, Emission Spectrum, and Absorption Spectrum. Noah's rainbow is a Continuous Spectrum. Neon signs, fluorescent lights, and Nebulas create an Emission Spectrum. Kepler's global network of ground-based telescopes is employing the science of Absorption Spectrum. It is this spectrum that excites planet

---

[35] Ibid.; Robinson, Keith. *Spectroscopy: The Key to the Stars.* Springer-Verlag: London, 2007. Print. (p.1)

hunters the most, for this spectrum reveals what most scientists thought impossible for centuries. If light waves from a star we can see have travelled through the atmosphere of a planet, its rainbow spectrum will show black lines where some of the light waves of the rainbow were absorbed. Those absorbed colors reveal the specific gases in that planet's atmosphere. By viewing these rainbows with their black absorption lines, astronomers can then identify what gases exist in the atmosphere of that alien world. In order for Kepler to identify these special light waves, it must look for stars that have planets eclipsing them relative to our line of sight. These eclipses are known as Transits.

Kepler's Specialty—Transits

Kepler's observation of these 156,000 stars around the Northern Cross is for the purpose of identifying solar eclipses. A solar eclipse is when a planet moves between us and its star, like when our Moon moves between us and our Sun. NASA calculates that a planet the size of Earth that passes in front of a star the size of our Sun at a distance as far away as the Northern Cross, will only dip in brightness about one-hundredth of a percent (.01%). This is equivalent to a pin passing in front of a 100 watt light bulb and the dip in brightness being noticed about 300 miles away. To make sure it is a true dip in brightness, Kepler must stare at these same 156,000 stars for four or more years to confirm regular cycles of dips. These dips in brightness might occur every week, every month, once a year or more depending on how often the object makes one revolution around its star. NASA mandated a four year mission (2009–2013) for the express purpose of identifying planets that eclipse their star once an Earth year.[36] Since NASA requires three

---

[36] Because of Kepler's great success, NASA extended its four year mission for an additional two years. In its fifth year of observation,

confirmed dips in brightness, the mission must last a minimum of three years and to be safe, four years. Kepler then transmits all the flagged planet candidates back to Earth about every three months. These candidates will then be assaulted with powerful ground-based telescopes to confirm or debunk them as planets to a 99.9999% accuracy. The ground-based telescopes also employ Spectral Analysis.

It is ironic how Spectral Analysis dominates astronomy today and plays such a critical role in the understanding of our universe, yet famous French philosopher, August Comte, declared to his students and respected international peers in 1835:

> *We understand the possibility for determining their shapes, their distances, their sizes and their movements; whereas we would never know how to study by any means their chemical composition...I persist in the opinion that every notion of the true mean temperatures of the stars will necessarily always be concealed from us.*[37]

Spectral Analysis broke through this concealment. The Kepler Spacecraft is taking this old science to a whole new level. The Kepler Mission is proving to be a mile-

---

2013, a second gyroscopic reaction wheel failed causing the ultimate end to Kepler's historic mission. However, it will take NASA's Kepler Science Team and network of ground-based telescopes years to scrutinize all the planet candidates, confirm which of these are within their habitable zone, and which of those are Earth's twin.

[37] Hearnshaw, J.B. *The Analysis of Starlight: One Hundred and Fifty Years of Astronomical Spectroscopy.* Cambridge University Press Syndicate: New York, 1986. Print (p.1). Robinson, Keith. *Spectroscopy: The Key to the Stars.* Springer: London, 2007. Print. (p.1)

marker in human history. For the first time, humans have the capability to discover, not just the chemical composition of stars, but of what orbits those stars.

Just imagine whole new worlds with warm climates, land, and water. One can't help but wonder how many other Earths Kepler has discovered in such a small sliver of space; a space that makes up only $1/400^{th}$ of our galaxy. And how many more worlds could that mean when considering the rest of the galaxies in our seeable universe…this is where we must go next.

2. HABITABLE WORLDS

The universe is not only queerer than we suppose, but queerer than we can suppose.[38]

~J.B.S. Haldane
(1892–1964)
Geneticist/Biologist/Atheist

If a planet is too close to its star, like Venus and Mercury, water will evaporate. If the planet is too far from its star, like Mars and Jupiter, then water remains frozen solid. The zone around a star where water remains liquid is known as the Habitable Zone, or as some astronomers call it, "the Goldilocks Zone," for it's just right—not too hot and not too cold.[39] Since this writing, ground-based telescopes alone have discovered over 700 new worlds, known as exoplanets, but none within their habitable zone. Kepler has already identified 3,548 planet candidates. NASA has confirmed 150 of these as planets and expect the great majority to also be confirmed. So of the 150 confirmed to date, 5 of them are just right—within their star's habitable zone.[40] Five habitable planets out of the 150 confirmed planets is an impressive 3%. If we use this percentage against the remaining 3,548 planet candidates, that is an additional 116 planets within their star's habitable zone. These amazing findings are causing the astronomical

---

[38] Ferris, Timothy. "Worlds Apart." *National Geographic Magazine*, December 2009. Print. (p.91)
[39] Jayawardhana, Ray. "Are Super-Sized Earths the New Frontier?" *Astronomy*, November 2008 (Volume 36, Issue 11).
[40] Watch the count online at JPLs' Kepler Mission website: www.planetquest.jpl.nasa.gov

community to shift their age-old thinking that perhaps planets and solar systems aren't the exception, but the rule.[41] This is a monumental swing in the way humans think of the heavens and our place in it. This mission will forever do away with the long standing assumption that stars are just lonely pin-points of light. Instead, kids will see them as Suns of other worlds.

Kepler's Ramifications

If NASA's Kepler science team is correct, Earth is far from being one-of-a-kind. They estimate that Kepler is not just going to discover other planets, nor just other habitable planets, but fifty or more other Earths.[42] Worlds just like our Earth in size, density, orbital period—Earth's twin. Think about it...actual worlds just like ours in every way. This would be a "Christopher Columbus" moment! Such incredible news will circulate the globe overnight and stir the imaginations and conversations of people everywhere. Christians around the world will have varying responses to these alien Earths: Some will doubt the news and remain ardent skeptics, others will embrace it finding the idea exciting, and still other Christians will demonize it claiming it just another trick from the Father of Lies. But all Christians will ponder the meaning of such amazing discoveries. Many will begin to wonder how to assimilate this information into their belief in God's Word since it is silent about such things. It begs the question, is our faith ready for what was unseen is now being seen?

---

[41] Jayawardhana, Ray. "Are Super-Sized Earths the New Frontier?" *Astronomy*, November 2008 (Volume 36, Issue 11).
[42] FAQ section in NASA's Kepler website, question #7 on how many other earths will be found and when. Go to: http://kepler.nasa.gov/Mission/faq/#a7

> *And when you look up to the sky and see the sun, the moon and the stars--all the heavenly array... (Deuteronomy 4:19a).*

Those countless lights teasing you from above are almost exactly the way they were when Adam and Eve first looked up at them, when Moses killed a man and then ran alone into the desert with those same stars to guide him, that our revolutionary leader, Jesus Christ, cried out to in His most despairing moments, and that the Apostle Paul escaped under on his church-planting missions across the Roman Empire. These are the same ancient stars we see today and forever captured on historic photographic plates at the Mt. Palomar Observatory.

Palomar Observatory

A lonely stretch of two-lane road takes you to the foot of the Palomar Mountain Range where you'll find a switchback road hugging the mountainside all the way up to the summit. Parking the car and walking the last hundred yards, I could see the massive Palomar Observatory like a Cyclops looming over the trees and rock. I walked over feeling silently giddy, being at such a historic place that I've only ever seen on TV and movies; a place I've dreamed of as a boy. Palomar's 200 inch diameter Pyrex mirror was cutting-edge technology in the 1930s, taking thirteen years to fabricate and polish, and almost never finished because of World War II. The "Giant Eye" as American newspapers called it, traveled slowly by railroad and truck from New York to San Diego, with people flocking to see it from coast to coast. It captured the pride of America. Walking around the outside of the circular structure, I stopped near the western-most "side" to soak in the warm sun and think about the decades of astronomy and famous persons that have been here like Carl Sagan. Lifting my hand to shield my eyes from the brilliant sunshine, it became immediately apparent why this spot was chosen. Like a lighthouse on a cliff overlooking the ocean, Palomar looks over every mountain as far as the eye can see all the way to the distant western horizon.

As I lingered, from around the observatory hobbles an older gentleman, hands in the pockets of his dark blue trousers and wearing a dark blue shirt topped off with a royal-blue Navy cap showing off a shiny gold medal on it. His face had seen many years, but good years from the gentleness in his demeanor. He begins recounting to me the story of how he, a young sailor, was there in '47 when the forty ton mirror crawled up the side of the mountain. While talking, he turned and pointed to a bunch of overgrowth and trees where apparently a road used to be: "The trucks came up 'this way' with the mirror on one and two trucks behind it...couldn't be going more than a few mph." History, in that moment, came to life.

Not only was Palomar the first scope to see the very edge of our seeable universe, but it also mapped the heavens known as the Palomar Plates Sky Survey. This foundational survey of the Northern Hemisphere of the Cosmos became the international road map for most of the twentieth century and still referred to today. Since this survey, Palomar's Caltech and the University of Massachusetts produced an even more ambitious one called The Two Micron All Sky Survey (2MASS) at the turn of this century. During this four year time frame (1997–2001), they captured the northern and southern hemispheres revealing what looks like a web of lights instead of points of light like what we're accustomed to seeing:

OTHER EARTHS / ALIEN LIFE
CHAPTER TWO – HABITABLE WORLDS

This landmark map made it into scientific journals, publications, and popular magazines around the world, for the web of lights you see are not stars, but galaxies. This startling image[43] reveals just how massive our universe is with estimates running as high as over 100 billion galaxies in just our local universe (image courtesy of 2MASS/UMass/IPAC-Caltech/NASA/NSF). Think about that a moment if you dare. Let it sink in—100 billion galaxies (100,000,000,000). Now multiply that by a rough average of 200 billion stars per galaxy. What is the probability of planets, within a star's habitable zone, when you consider it like this?

And these are only the galaxies we can see. Astronomers have shown that the farther away the galaxy, the greater its Doppler red shift. The Doppler red shift is caused when light speeds away from us. All light, when bent through a prism, reveals a rainbow of colors, like a rainbow seen in the sky. The farther and faster light is speeding away from Earth, that rainbow spectrum of light will shift toward the red. The greater the red shift the farther and faster it is speeding away. Galaxies show the greatest red shifts. They are the farthest from us and moving the fastest away from us as documented at the

---

[43] To view this stunning image, go +to the University of Massachusetts website: <http://pegasus.astro.umass.edu/image_gallery/allsky.jpg.>

Palomar and Lick Observatories. In this composite image of galaxies, the farthest galaxies have accelerated to the brink of the speed of light; no galaxies can be seen beyond this point because its light has shifted too far into the red beyond our visible-light spectrum. Thus astronomers refer to everything that we can see and detect as our "local universe" or "seeable universe," which they approximate to be roughly 13.7 billion light years away from us in every direction North, South, East, and West.[44] To clarify "universe," whenever any astronomer uses this word, they are usually only referring to our local, seeable universe. Beyond our local universe, space is believed to go on and on and on with even more galaxies, at least, that is the assumption.

What astronomers have desired since the telescope was first invented in 1608[45] and put to Galileo's eye in 1610, is bigger and bigger scopes to see farther and farther away. Galileo's telescope had an aperture (diameter) of around 1 inch but a practical and usable aperture of only ½ an inch due to the poor lens quality around the periphery of the lenses. Today's largest scope, the Large Binocular Telescope (LBT), hosts twin mirrors, like binoculars, totaling 464 inches (11.8 meters) in aperture; but even this telescope will soon be eclipsed by the whopping 1,181 inch (30 meters) Binocular Telescope in Chile with first light projected to be in 2018. That is 1,181 times the light gathering power from the days of Galileo. But ironically,

---

[44] www.pbs.org/wgbh/nova/universe/howbig.html. It is an estimate, at best.

[45] At least, this is when the first patent was submitted for it by Hans Lipperhey from the Netherlands and known as a "humble and God-Fearing man . Many designs with different names were use before this in China, Greece, Arabia, and Europe but Hans Lipperhey in the Netherlands was the first to submit a patent on it and so given the title of the inventor of the telescope, but it is Galileo Galilei in 1610 whom made the telescope famous with his observations of the heavens.

beginning with the "Giant Eye" on Mt. Palomar, astronomers cannot see any further away. They have already reached the cliff of our visible universe, seeing as far as the red shift allows. Larger telescopes may not be able to see any farther away, but they can see better. These massive telescopes today are more like microscopes to dissect the universe in stunning detail, teasing out the light reflecting off exoplanets orbiting distant stars and soon to be able to even measure the gases in their atmospheres.

So Let's Do The Numbers

We know from the most recent observations with NASA's Spitzer Space Telescope that Andromeda galaxy has roughly one trillion stars and our Milky Way has about four hundred billion.[46] This, by the way, is a great illustration of how cosmologists can be tremendously wrong in their figures since they estimated just ten years ago that these two galaxies had half this number of stars in them. With this in mind, let's play it conservative, and instead of using our Milky Way's 400 billion stars, let's cut that in half and use 200 billion as the average number of stars in each galaxy across our universe. I do this since there are multiple dwarf galaxies and irregular galaxies around each large galaxy and they have much fewer stars. Multiply this conservative rough estimate by the estimated 100 billion galaxies in our seeable universe and this still equals a whopping 20 trillion billion stars (20,000,000,000,000,000,000,000)[47] just in our seeable universe.

---

[46] Some say as many as 500 billion stars. The diameter of the Milky Way galaxy alone is 100,000 light years. It is now believed that the Milky Way is actually similar in size to the Andromeda Galaxy, our closest major neighbor, which we used to think not 15 years ago was twice our size. You can see Andromeda with your naked eye on a clear, dark, moonless night once your eyes adjust.

Now take the 3,548 worlds discovered (all these candidate planets are expected to be confirmed) out of the 156,000 stars Kepler observed to get a rough ratio of 1 planet out of every 43 stars observed. Good ol' fashioned arithmetic is all that is needed now to get a rough idea of how many planets could exist across our galaxy and even across our universe:

- 200 billion star galaxy divided by 43 stars/planet equals over 4 billion 600 million planets in each average size galaxy.

- The Milky Way galaxy with its 400 billion stars, comes to over 9 billion 300 million planets.

- Across our entire universe of 100 billion galaxies multiplied by an average galaxy comes to over 460 billion billion (460,000,000,000,000,000,000) planets in our seeable universe.

This is a severely over-simplistic calculation, especially in light of Dr. Frank Drake's famous equation on habitable worlds and alien life presented at the Green Bank Conference in 1960.[48] But. Even if I am off by an embarrassing ninety-nine percent—that one percent still means over 46 million planets exist in each average galaxy and over 93 million planets in the Milky Way galaxy!

Now factor in that out of Kepler's 150 confirmed planets, 5 of them are in their star's habitable zone. That is

---

[47] A trillion billion is also known as a sextillion. So 20 Sextillion stars.
[48] Goto www.PBS.org and select "Origins" and then select "The Drake Equation." The equation: $N = R^* \times f_p \times n_e \times f_l \times f_i \times f_c \times L$. Dr. Frank Drake is Professor Emeritus for Astronomy and Astrophysics at the University of California, Santa Cruz.

an impressive 3%. Meaning that out of the 93 million-plus planets that may exist in our Milky Way, 2 million 790 thousand (2,790,000) worlds might be in their star's habitable zone. And what if I'm another 99% in error on this estimate...that still means 27,900 habitable zone planets exist in our Milky Way. Just imagine, potential habitable worlds with pristine oceans of water, snow-capped mountains, and warm comfortable climates. But this cold, hard math is, well...really cold and hard.

Open vs. Closed Universe

Christian faith proclaims that cold, hard math is not how our Universe was created. Math and Physics were used, yes, but by whom, not just how and when. It is well within God's jurisdiction to allow just physics to dictate the number of habitable planets in our seeable universe or to bypass physics all together and create whatever He wants. Let me frame it this way, which is more probable: Was it probable for the blind man to see? No, but he did. Was it probable for the man crippled since birth to walk? No, but he did. How about Peter stepping out of the boat and walking on water (well...for a few steps anyway)—how probable was that? And herein lies the hubris of mathematicians and astrophysicists. Pierre Simon marquis de Laplace (1749–1827), a highly celebrated French mathematician and astronomer, was crucial in the development of applied mathematical astronomy and overtly proclaimed the universe was mechanistic. Meaning that everything could be predicted—right down to human behavior.[49] Scientists call this "scientific determinism" while philosophers refer to it as "fatalism" and Christian theologians classify this notion as a "closed universe." It is

---

[49] Hawking, Stephen. *A Brief History of Time*. A Bantam Book: New York, 1996. Print

these views espoused by atheists and so well-articulated in this famous quote:

> *That Man is the product of causes which had no pre-vision of the end they were achieving; that his origin, his growth, his hopes and fears, his loves and his beliefs, are but the outcome of accidental collocations of atoms; that no fire, no heroism, no intensity of thought and feeling, can preserve an individual life beyond the grave. ...[we] are destined to extinction in the vast death of the solar system, and the whole temple of Man's achievement must inevitably be buried beneath the debris of a universe in ruins.*[50]

These fatalistic notions assume the Universe is nothing more than a chaos-driven mechanism destined to destruction. This destruction begins with our Sun going Nova and swallowing the Earth.[51] Then billions of years later the Andromeda galaxy finally slams into the Milky Way ripping it apart. And then finally, billions of years after that, the universe expands into oblivion so the smallest atomic sub-particle is light years from one another.[52] While other close-minded cosmologists share the same hopelessness but with a different end-time theory. They

---

[50] Bertrand, Russell. *Mysticism and Logic.* New York: Norton, 1929. Print. (pp47-48, 56-57)

[51] A star of 8 solar masses (our Sun is 1 solar mass) or less will die going Nova leaving a Planetary Nebula in its wake like the famous M57 Ring Nebula. A star with 8 solar masses or more will go Supernova ending as a Neutron Star or Pulsar. A star above 25 solar masses may infinitely collapse into a Black Hole or become a magnetar.

[52] Heat death is the death of hear caused by entropy. It is our universe's theorized ultimate end.

teach that the universe will expand only so far then reverse direction and collapse back upon itself causing another Big Bang over and over and over.[53] In either case, scientists with a closed universe mentality are saying we are all victims of fate and that there is absolutely nothing we can do about anything. Such fatalistic notions have no space for the idea of hope, miracles, or a God that caringly intervenes.

Biblical faith is exactly opposite of fatalism. Christian faith believes in an Open Universe,[54] the belief that God intervenes in our space-time and in our lives upsetting the natural order with the super-natural. Every time God intervenes somewhere in the universe, He is upsetting that clock-like mechanism that would have otherwise left us to cold, hard math. We as Christians don't believe in fate; we believe in miracles. Miracles can only come from someone outside our universe, beyond the math and physics powering this natural order.

Since legitimate science needs measurable and repeatable proofs before it recognizes something to be true, the countless miracles experienced and witnessed throughout human existence should be more than enough measurable proof that we live in an Open Universe. And in an Open Universe, anything is possible: *"Jesus looked at them and said, 'With man this is impossible, but with God all things are possible'" (Matthew 19:26).*

Ground based telescopes are now discovering new worlds almost weekly but cannot resolve planets as small as Earth; but Kepler can. Humanity now has the capability to finally know if worlds like Earth orbit stars like our Sun.

---

[53] Hawking, Stephen. *A Brief History of Time*. A Bantam Book: New York, 1996. Print
[54] Do not confuse this with Open Theism.

And as NASA's Kepler Science Team scrutinizes all the planet candidates Kepler has discovered, the count of habitable worlds will grow. And just how many of these are just like Earth is the exciting question they will indeed answer soon enough.

3. THE ROAD TO THIS PIVOTAL MOMENT

> *'Come now, let us reason together,'* says the LORD.
> ~Isaiah 1:18

A dark cave in Lascaux, France betrays its treasure only once a year during a few fleeting minutes on the shortest day, Winter Solstice. This is when our Sun travels at its lowest along the southern horizon. It is around this day when sunlight shines through the cave to sneak a peek at a wall deep within. On this wall, sketch-art dating back to the days of Adam & Eve are illuminated.[55] These ancient sketches capture stick-people clutching spears held above there heads hunting an animal. As this painting so well illustrates, we have been keenly aware of the heavenly motions like when Winter Solstice occurs, since God breathed life into us, ushering in the age of humans. On such a disconcerting day when our ancestors feared darkness winning over light, they immortalized the most important of events—the slaying of an animal for human survival.

Authors in scripture also reveal a keen awareness to the heavens in the opening lines of Genesis, *"In the beginning God created the heavens and the earth"*

---

[55] Carbon 14 dating, potassium-argon dating, thermo-luminescent dating, sedimentary dating, Lead isotope dating all employ the scientific method for processing and analyzing. The problem comes in the historical assumptions made by scientist, a subjective exercise, of what the specimen was exposed to over the centuries and millenia in order to make their age conclusions. This is also true for Antarctic ice rod samples and ocean floor rod samples. Scientists are able to draw general conclusions perhaps, but not precise reviews of actual history.

(Genesis 1:1), and having crossed thousands of years, numerous continents, documenting the rise and fall of empires in human history, the Bible then ends with the same attention given to the heavens:

> *Then I saw a new heaven and a new earth, for the first heaven and the first earth had passed away (Revelation 21:1–2).*

The Cosmos are constantly on the minds of humans and God, as seen in the Bible and world history.

Stonehenge, was founded about four thousand years ago (around 3,000 B.C.–2,500 B.C.) by a lost race using it to mark the positions of the Sun, stars, and Moon. The Tower of Babel[56] was erected with the heavens in mind along with the Great Pyramid of Giza in the same rough period of lost history, all highlighting the ageless obsession we have with the heavenly wonders—the Moon, Sun, planets, and stars.[57] Of all the stars, the North Star, named Polaris, is unique, because of its perspective from Northern Latitudes. It is the one prominent star that doesn't seem to move. It can always be seen no matter the season while all the other stars appear to rise from the east and set in the west as the Earth rotates, yet the North Star remains. It is this star Leif Ericson and Christopher Columbus and all sea-faring captains to this day have relied on for navigation. It is this unchanging star the Pyramid architects and

---

[56] Chapters 1–11 in Genesis are commonly known among biblical scholars as primeval history or pre-history since these events were celebrated in oral tradition only from generation to generation. The written word had not yet existed. Archeologists and biblical scholars providing dates on the building of the Tower of Babel (Genesis 11:1–9) are estimates at best…even those who claim to have located and excavated the ziggurat that they believe to be the Tower of Babel.

[57] Magli, Giulio. *Mysteries And Discoveries of Archaeoastronomy.* Praxis Publishing: New York, 2009. Print.

workers believed to be the very gateway to heaven, the abode of the gods.[58] I point all this out to highlight how humans, since the dawn of Creation, have yearned and strived and accomplished seemingly impossible feats with the Cosmos in mind. As they learned, they were paving the way for this epic mission executed by NASA to answer these age old questions that have obsessed our ancestors for thousands of years...well before light from these 156,000 stars even began the journey to us.

The Beginning Of The Road

Ancient civilizations relied on the brilliant minds of their time to understand and explain complex things such as why daylight grows shorter and then longer, why some "stars" streak through the night and others appear to slowly wander and even reverse direction, which we know today to be planets. The tendency of modern civilization is to overlook our forefather's accomplishments, before modern science, forgetting that it is these men of old who prepared the groundwork for laying the road to modern science. Forefathers like the Ionian scientist named Pythagoras in the 6th century.[59] He gave us the famous Pythagorean theorem for math, which is taught in high school today. And Plato, who inspired Johannes Kepler to embrace Copernicus' revolutionary theory by teaching,

> ...[the] heavens being a reflection of a perfect order and harmony of the highest levels of mind and beauty—the realm of ideas.[60]

---

[58] Magli, Giulio. *Mysteries And Discoveries of Archaeoastronomy.* Praxis Publishing: New York, 2009. Print.

[59] Ironically, Pythagorean Theorem is his contribution to science to this day in math, and he was one of the first known scholars to promote the idea that the Earth moves and is not immobile.

Like their forefathers, the fathers of modern science held to the age-old belief that studying the cosmos is no less than entering into the realm of God's creativeness, being able to see the handiwork and fingerprints of God. It was a way of knowing our Creator and ourselves better by learning about His Creation and our place in it. This worldview was that of Copernicus, Galileo, Kepler, and Newton who pioneered modern science, astronomy, and the laws that govern NASA's Kepler Spacecraft.

NASA's Mission Inspiration

The road to this pivotal moment in science and astronomy started with Nicolaus Copernicus (1473–1543), a brilliant Polish priest[61] who studied the stars from the comfort and solitude of his tower-house in Frombork, Poland. It is in this castle fortress where he documented his naked-eye observations and wrote himself into history. As mentioned earlier, he established his controversial theory that the Earth is not the center of the universe. He carefully entrusted copies of his work to loyal friends and wrote it only in Latin so as not to fall into the hands of the masses. With much encouragement from his confidants, Copernicus released his book for printing but only on his deathbed. He knew the dim view his colleagues in the Roman Catholic Church would have on his book. It was this book that heavily influenced many of the fathers of modern science, including Galileo Galilei and Johannes Kepler.

---

[60] Jones, Roger S. *Physics for the Rest of Us*. Contemporary Books: Chicago, 1992. Print. (p.128)
[61] Nicolaus Copernicus (1473 A.D.–1543 A.D.). First astronomer to establish mathematical proofs on the motion of the Earth around the Sun, known as the helio-centric solar system. The Roman Catholic Church only very recently recognized Copernicus and his work.

It took over a hundred years before Galileo Galilei (1564–1642)[62] in Italy and Johannes Kepler (1571–1630) in today's Germany would continue Copernicus' work. Galileo's many accomplishments would earn him the title, Father of Modern Science and Kepler the Father of Planetary Motion.

Galileo was a highly intelligent, albeit arrogant, man who eventually agreed with Copernicus' findings and put it so in print with a title boldly challenging not just the long-standing cosmological model of Ptolemy, but the very beliefs of the Holy Roman Catholic Church: *Dialogue Concerning The Two Chief World Systems: Ptolemaic and Copernican* (1632). To make matters worse, instead of publishing the book in Latin, the language of scholars and the elite, he had it published in common Italian so as to be readable by the most people possible.[63] One man stood against the mighty Roman Catholic Church…and lost. Sentenced by the Inquisition to lifelong house arrest, Galileo was forced to recant his views of the Earth orbiting the Sun, dying blind, uncelebrated, and buried in a private funeral by the church. In 1992, 350 years later, Pope John Paul II formally recognized the error of the Church in condemning Galileo.[64]

Johannes Kepler (1571–1630)

Galileo's fate did not befall the protestant, Johannes Kepler, whom NASA named this mission after, and might be one of NASA's many faux pas. Kepler was a strange

---

[62] Father of Modern Science whom championed Copernicus' findings through his own book, *DIA'LOGO* (short for: *Dialogue Concerning the Two Chief World Systems*), published in 1632.
[63] Hawking, Stephen. *A Briefer History of Time.* Bantam Books: New York, 2005. Print. (p.146)
[64] http://www.nytimes.com/1992/11/01/world/vatican-science-panel-told-by-pope-galileo-was-right.html

boy with big round eyes, a prominent chin, and a short wiry frame, constantly struggling with ailments as a child.[65] Astrophysicist Marcelo Gleiser proclaims Kepler's life to be the most "colorful and tragic of the whole of science."[66] His life story is a movie producer's dream, an epic drama to be sure. I see the opening scene fading in from black, while the sound of yelling kids swells until you make out a rustling mob of boys kicking a weaker boy huddled up in the mud outside the school building. The young Kepler, used to such treatment, knows to protect himself while peeking out, anxious for a break between the gang's mess of legs. Seeing an opening, he scrambles out, running home only to be welcomed by a rage-filled father stomping out the door and a screaming mother throwing curses at his silhouette as he dissolves into the morning fog—never to be seen again.

Johannes Kepler was the firstborn of Katherine and Heinrich Kepler in the small town of Weil der Stadt, in today's Germany. Katherine followed the ways of her mother who was later burned at the stake for witchcraft.[67] His father, Heinrich, rarely stayed home and finally just disappeared, some say dying somewhere in the Netherlands as a mercenary soldier.[68] Kepler described his father as "destroying everything,"[69] "rough," and "immoral" and preferred him out of the house for the sake of keeping the peace.[70] Johannes was picked on often at school for his

---

[65] Voelkel, James. *Johannes Kepler and the New Astronomy*. Oxford University Press: Cary, 1999. Print.
[66] Frankenberry, Nancy. *The Faith of Scientists In Their Own Words*. Princeton University Press: Princeton, 2008. Print.
[67] Hawking, Stephen (edited and commentary). *On the Shoulders of Giants*. Running Press: Philadelphia, 2002. Print.
[68] Voelkel, James. *Johannes Kepler and the New Astronomy*. Oxford University Press: Cary, 1999. Print.
[69] Frankenberry, Nancy. *The Faith of Scientists In Their Own Words*. Princeton University Press: Princeton, 2008. Print.

small size and smarts.[71] He embraced books at a young age, being very inquisitive like his mother. His teachers noticed his intelligence early on, earning him a grant from Duke Ludwig to an all-boys college-prep school where he learned to write, speak, and read Latin, the language of scholars. Raised Lutheran, he began studies in theology at Tubingen University in 1587 with hopes to be a Lutheran theologian. His brilliance in math, however, caught the attention of math professor Michael Maestlin, who became his mentor not only through college but the rest of his life. Upon receiving his baccalaureate in 1588, Maestlin urged Duke Ludwig to award Kepler a scholarship for Stift, the Lutheran seminary. Upon completing his two years of seminary study, his teachers saw "great things in him"[72] and with the approval again of the Duke, awarded him an extended three year study in theology. Life, however, took an unexpected detour. The university caught wind that the Catholic Jesuits had set up a school in Graz, Austria, prompting the Protestants in Graz to set up a Protestant Seminary just down the road as a direct rebuttal. Desperate for teachers, the university pressured Kepler into taking the post as the District Math Professor at Graz. Kepler enjoyed the larger town of Tubingen and had his heart set on ministry, but out of respect for his mentor, the Duke, and the years of generosity funding his education, he felt obliged to accept the call and teach math in the small town of Graz.

A common duty of the district mathematician in that day was to produce the annual almanac and astrological calendar. Due to his mother, who practiced witchcraft, he was quite familiar with astrological practices and combined

---

[70] Voelkel, James. *Johannes Kepler and the New Astronomy*. Oxford University Press: Cary, 1999. Print.
[71] Ibid.
[72] Ibid.

it with his math brilliance to produce in 1595 an uncanny accuracy foretelling of the Muslim Ottoman Turks surprise attack to Austria's southern border, a bitterly cold winter, and a peasant uprising. This almanac caused the locals to hail him a prophet.[73] Constantly in need of a supplemental income, Kepler confessed to his longtime and disapproving mentor, *If God gave every animal tools for maintaining life, what harm is there if for the same purpose He joined astrology to astronomy?*[74] Even though Kepler continued providing astrological predictions for pay throughout his life, he referred to astrology as, *the foolish little daughter of astronomy.*[75] But, being popular in the middle ages, astrology produced fast money for him and his family.

Kepler married twice, his first wife, Barbara Muller for twelve years, whom fell ill after a Bohemian invasion dying shortly after in 1611. She bore him six children with only two surviving to adulthood. When three of them died from illness within a six month period, Kepler confessed this to be the lowest point in his life. His second wife, Susanna Ruttinger, bore him seven more children with only two surviving to adulthood. Kepler never fully recovered from the loss of his children, and found much solace in his obsession to reveal the Trinity in the Copernican theory of the universe.

The pivotal moment in his life, his epiphany, occurred during one of his math classes on July 19, 1595. He explains that he was drawing a circle around a triangle with the circle touching the three points of the triangle when he saw the model of the universe (our solar system)

---

[73] Hawking, Stephen. (edited and commentary). *On the Shoulders of Giants*. Running Press: Philadelphia, 2002. Print.
[74] Voelkel, James. *Johannes Kepler and the New Astronomy*. Oxford University Press: Cary, 1999. Print. (p.27)
[75] Ibid.

and the Trinity harmoniously together. The Trinity was so central in Kepler's Christian worldview, he set out to prove how the image of God is revealed in the making of the universe where the planets orbit (circles) about the Trinity (triangles). His first book developed the argument that the Sun symbolizes God the Father, fixed and unmovable, at the center of the universe (Copernacism) with a force drawing all things to it (we now know as gravity) with the Earth as being wholly unique in all the Cosmos as is Christ the Son, and the Spirit filling the intervening space (Aristotle's Aether).[76] Kepler *wept tears of joy*[77] upon this discovery, calling it a *stupendous miracle of God*.[78] And this epiphany became Kepler's first published book, filled with complex geometrical relation and mathematical proofs to explain the motions of the known planets titled, *Mystery of the Cosmos* in 1597. He sent this book to numerous scholars of math and theology including a then little known Italian math teacher named Galileo Galilei. Although Galileo did not respond at that time due to the distractions of a young love interest, he did take time to cite Kepler's math and theology as interesting but lacking proof. One astronomer, however, a nobleman from Denmark exiled to Prague, did respond: Tycho Brahe.[79]

Brahe and Kepler might as well be "A" and "Z" in the alphabet or "North" and "South" on a compass; polar opposites in nearly every way—the boisterous Brahe and the quiet Kepler, the elitist Brahe and the boy from little means, the Catholic and the Protestant, the center of the Universe Brahe and the Copernican Kepler. With but two

---

[76] Frankenberry, Nancy. *The Faith of Scientists in Their Own Words*. Princeton University Press: Princeton, 2008. Print.
[77] Voelkel, James. *Johannes Kepler and the New Astronomy*. Oxford University Press: Cary, 1999. Print. (p.33)
[78] Ibid
[79] Ibid.

exceptions: equal life obsessions in understanding the motions of the heavens matched only by their equal desires for immortality in history. Theirs would prove a tumultuous working relationship filled with mistrust, fits of rage, and culminating in the untimely death of Brahe.

Brahe was impressed with Kepler's math and offered him an assistant position at his new cutting-edge observatory in Benatky Castle to help him revise the fifteen hundred year old Ptolemaic cosmological system and thus renaming it: *The Tychonic Laws of Planetary Motion*. Brahe's research and observatory were funded by the Holy Roman Emperor whose interest was to combat the Sun-centered model of Copernicus. What drew Kepler to Brahe was Brahe's priceless 20-volume set of precise movements of the planets collected over a 35 year period kept in mammoth books known as the *Rudolphine Tablets*, named after the emperor. These tablets contained planetary motions to an unprecedented accuracy of 2 arc minutes—though Brahe commonly bragged of an accuracy of 1 arc minute (1/60th of a degree). His measurements would prove upto thirty times more accurate than any data on planetary positions at that time. So the stage was set: Brahe was paranoid that Kepler was out to steal his data; and mad-jealousy on Kepler's part for not being allowed free access to the data. The story then takes a Stephen King twist with the very untimely death of Brahe one and a half years later. Whether or not Kepler was involved in Brahe's death is still debated to this day. Both in 1901 and again in 2010, Brahe's body was exhumed to undergo forensics on Brahe's hair, which showed at the turn of the 20th century high levels of calcium and mercury.[80]

---

[80] "Tycho Brahe to be exhumed." *The Copenhagen Post*. Feb 4, 2010. Retrieved May 27, 2010, Wikipedia, August 9, 2010; "Digging up Brahe." *The Prague Post*. May 12, 2010. Retrieved May 27, 2010. Wikipedia, August 9, 2010.

Milk was a common medium for poisoning by drink in that era and Kepler had complete access to Brahe's alchemy lab and self-educated in it. It seemed Kepler had the motive and means but one may never really know.[81] What we do know is that Brahe's planetary data was priceless to Kepler, moving the scrappy Kepler to try and acquire it in many ways, both honest and devious. This letter he wrote to his mentor and confidant, Maestlin, could certainly be used against him:

> *Let all keep silence and hark to Tycho who has devoted thirty-five years to his observations. For Tycho alone do I wait; he shall explain to me the order and arrangement of the orbits. Then I hope I shall one day, if God keeps me alive, erect a wonderful edifice. ...Brahe may discourage me from Copernicus (or even from the five perfect solids) but rather I think about striking Tycho himself with a sword. I think thus about Tycho: he abounds in riches, which like most rich people he does not rightly use. Therefore great effort has to be given that we may wrest his riches away from him. (Letter to Michael Maestlin, February 16 1599, Gesammelte Werke, vol. xiii, (p. 289).[82]*

---

[81] Sungenis, Robert A. *Oh What Tangled Webs We Weave: The Personal Lives and Philosophies of Copernicus, Kepler, Galileo, Newton and Einstein.* [CD] <http://www.catholicintl.com/noncatholicissues/personal_lives.htm.>
[82] Ibid.

NASA's Faux Pas

Without this crucial data, he would be nothing more than an astrologer, math teacher, and Brahe's assistant. When Brahe suddenly came ill with abdominal pains and died two days later, Kepler, by his own confession, did not wait for approval from the family nor the Holy Roman Emperor funding the *Rudolphine Tablets* but acquired them "without delay."[83] A year later, Kepler announced the discovery of the first two laws of planetary motion and published them two years later titled, *New Astronomy* (1609). The First Law: The planets move in elliptical orbits, with the Sun at one focus. Second Law: The line connecting the planet and the Sun sweeps out in equal areas in equal times. The observational data combined with the geometrical illustrations and mathematical proofs proved indisputable and made Kepler famous. Brahe's death also positioned Kepler as the new Imperial Mathematician in Prague—causing even Galileo to seek Kepler's scholarly advice. In 1604 a bright burning Super-Nova was named *Kepler's Nova*.[84] Kepler's third and final law of planetary motion came out nine years later in 1618 in his series of five books combining astronomy, theology, philosophy, and mysticism titled, *Harmonies of the World*. The Third Law: The square of the orbital period of a planet is proportional to the cube of the semi-major axis of its orbit. It was this third and final law that laid the detailed groundwork for Sir Isaac Newton, sixty years later, to establish the law of gravity. Upon Kepler establishing these three laws, filled with emotion near the end of his life, he writes:

---

[83] Voelkel, James. *Johannes Kepler and the New Astronomy*. Oxford University Press: Cary, 1999. Print.
[84] Hawking, Stephen (edited and commentary). *On The Shoulders of Giants*. Running Press: Philadelphia, 2002. Print.

> *I dare frankly to confess that I have stolen the golden vessels of the Egyptians to build a tabernacle for my God far from the bounds of Egypt. If you pardon me, I shall rejoice; if you reproach me, I shall endure. The die is cast, and I am writing the book, to be read either now or by posterity, it matters not. It can wait a century for a reader, as God himself has waited six thousand years for a witness.*

Johannes Kepler's three laws unlock the secrets to all worlds no matter how distant the star they orbit. But it seems to me, NASA failed to consider Tycho's key role when naming this history-making mission that future students around the world will read about in their history books. It seems to me they should have named it: The Tycho-Kepler Spacecraft.

PART II

ALIEN LIFE

I do not feel obliged to believe that the same God who has endowed us with sense, reason, and intellect has intended us to forgo their use.

~Galileo Galilei
(1564–1642)

4. WHERE THE ROAD LEADS NEXT

> *...those of us who represent social organization and political institutions look upon you [science] with a feeling that includes much of awe and something of fear as we ask ourselves to what revolution you will next require us to adapt our scheme of human relations.*[85]
>
> ~Calvin Coolidge, 30th President
> December 30, 1924

If there were a road sign for the chapters to follow, it would be the yellow flashing caution sign depicting road curves, since mind-bending concepts are just 'round the corner. Although these chapters to follow will prove the most intriguing and challenging, I also believe they will prove the most rewarding, coming away from this book deeply encouraged in your faith. It is my belief you will more fully appreciate just how transcendent God is and how limitless His creativeness can be. But in order to stay "between the lines" instead of crashing through the guard rails of sound theology and proven science, we must first consider some key concepts in physics and theology. So before we take on the curves ahead, let's slow down to get a "feel for the road" here in this chapter. For without heeding the caution sign, the chapters to follow will feel more like sci-fi than sci-fact.

---

[85] Bartusiak, Marcia. *The Day We Found the Universe*. Pantheon Books: New York, 2009. Print. (p.X) [brackets mine]

Duality

The idea of duality wars with our finite mind's ability to comprehend, for it exists at the outer edge of our reality, an alien place where space-time breaks down and common sense no longer rules. Duality is something that is and is not. In other words, it is something capable of being two different things at the same time. Sir Isaac Newton sparked a great debate on this concept when he proclaimed light to be a stream of particles while his contemporaries argued light to be a wave. This debate waxed and waned for over one hundred years until English physicist, Thomas Young (1773–1829), developed a now famous and oft repeated experiment called the Double-Slit Experiment, proving both sides were wrong and both sides were right. This experiment requires the use of an electron beam emitter, a receiver plate, and photographic film to catch the electrons emitted. Since Hobby Lobby™ is all out of them, we'll have to come up with another way of doing Young's experiment. Let's use hockey. Imagine you are a famous hockey player, like the Great One, Wayne Gretzky. Snatching the puck from your opponent, you race down the ice on a fast break, spurred on by the roar of a cheering crowd, adrenaline pumping, you pull away from your opponents and spy your chance to score. Almost instinctively you raise the hockey stick to smack the puck and with a sharp crack, the puck shoots into the air straight for the goal. The puck is that electron and your hockey stick is the electron emitter while the goal is the receiver plate. But instead of one goal, there are two side-by-side goals and this is where Young discovered the unbelievable. The puck goes into both goals simultaneously. When the goalie turns around to see if the puck made it into the net, what he finds is no longer a puck but a wave. The puck morphed on him. This is what Young's famous Double-Slit Experiment reveals with electrons. The electron seems to morph. Common sense tells you that a puck doesn't just change. But this is no ordinary puck. As if that isn't crazy enough, here is where the experiment enters the stuff of sci-fi. If one of the slits is closed, so only one slit is open, and you release another electron, this time the photographic film does not show a wave pattern but a single dot from one electron particle hitting the film like a bullet. Thomas Young's experiment revealed that an electron has a dual nature of being both a particle and a wave simultaneously. The experiment itself affects the characteristics of the electron. In other words, when one goal is on the ice rink, the puck stays a particle but when two goals are there, the puck changes into a wave in order to spread out and enter both goals simultaneously. This is famously known as the particle-wave duality of electrons.[86] Scientists were forced to accept the fact that they do not understand, and then stole a chapter from the brilliant minds of theologians seventeen hundred years earlier by embracing the concept of duality. Duality exists. This startling characteristic of electrons caused much consternation amongst classical physicists who expect nature to behave.[87] This experiment identified the first rebel particle, a particle that is both 100% particle and 100% wave.

Yet seventeen hundred years earlier, when light from a hundred thousand stars was still far, far away on its journey to Earth, this same debate on duality raged even more so by the brilliant minds of the day. One of Rome's last great leaders arose out of the far western lands of the empire that we know today to be France and Great Britain.

---

[86] Greene, Brian. *The Elegant Universe*. Vintage Books: New York, 2000. Print. (p.97)

[87] Richard Feynman has challenged this experiment with a quantum theory known as the Sum Over Histories, whereas the electron in the double-slit experiment tries all pathways simultaneously and that is what is being seen when both slits are open.

He reunites a weak and splintered empire under one rule and initiates the rise of the Holy Roman Catholic Church to ultimate power. It is during this age, duality got its start in western culture.

Constantine the Great (272 A.D.–337 A.D.) possessed the rare gift of knowing how to inspire troops and how to win battles others would never even attempt. His rise to power culminates at the *Battle of the Milvian Bridge* against Augustus Maxentius (312 A.D.), the emperor of the West. Outnumbered and tired, Constantine knows his troops need a miracle and he makes sure they get one. Days before the battle, he proclaims to his men a vision given to him during noontime prayer from God. As the revisionist Eusebius (263–339) writes,

> *He said that about noon, when the day was already beginning to decline, he saw with his own eyes the trophy of a cross of light in the heavens, above the sun, and bearing the inscription, CONQUER BY THIS.*[88]

Another historian, Lactantius (c. 240–c. 320) writes that Constantine had a dream that night: "…delineate the heavenly sign on the shields of his soldiers."[89] The symbol, that only Constantine saw, was the well-known and widely used *Chi-Rho* symbol, which is a Greek "X" (Chi) and "P" (Rho) layered on top of each other. By proclaiming he had seen this symbol above the Sun resonates with those in his army whom worship the popular roman Sun god, Sol

---

[88] Hebrews also associated this ancient symbol with time and God by placing the Alpha and Omega Greek letters on the left and right side of the Chi-Rho symbol.

[89] <http://en.wikipedia.org/wiki/Battle_of_the_Milvian_Bridge>

Invictus. By further proclaiming God gave him this sign, resonates with those whom follow Jesus Christ since the two Greek letters are the first two letters spelling "Christ" in the common language of Greek.[90] Capitalizing on this miraculous event before such a pivotal battle, his men have this symbol engraved on their shields. Legend holds that on the morning of the battle, Constantine himself wielded this symbol while riding a white horse in gleaming armor.[91] This gallant move fueled his outnumbered men to victory and Constantine to eventually become the new emperor of the West. Augustus Licinius, emperor of the East (which evolved into the Byzantine Empire), also adopted the *Chi-Rho* symbol for his troops as a proclamation that the God of Jesus Christ is on their side, and a way of showing goodwill toward the new western emperor. It is this symbol given to Constantine in his vision that becomes the forerunner of the Christian cross we know today. Without this vision, it is not clear if the cross would be associated with Christianity today or just remain a historic note of interest on cruel Roman execution methods.

As co-Emperors, Constantine in Rome and Licinius in Constantinople (today's Istanbul, Turkey), they co-authored the *Edict of Milan* mandating all persecutions against Christians to cease and all personal property be returned to them. This is the first formal step recognizing Christianity as a major religion in the Roman Empire. In later years, civil war broke out between the two emperors and Constantine defeated the larger army and navy of Licinius (324 A.D.) becoming the sole Emperor of the entire Roman world. As Constantine the Great, one of his first concerns was the unification of the empire and sees the schism threatening the young Christian religion as his

---

[90] Spelling Christ in ancient Greek is: "Χρήστος".
[91] Eusebius, *The History of the Church from Christ to Constantine*. Trans. G.A. Williamson. Dorset Press, NY: 1965. Print.

opportunity. Sealing letters with his royal ring, Constantine the Great dispatched messengers across his empire to seek out the best and brightest leaders of Christianity and present to them a formal invitation of the first roman ecumenical council to be held in Nicea, Turkey, 325 A.D. [92] The purpose of this council was to put to rest the divisive feud over Jesus Christ—is He God eternal or made by the eternal God. It was this moment, with this first publicly recognized ecumenical council,[93] that the secretive followers of Jesus Christ become accepted, mainstream, even celebrated. And by sponsoring this council, Constantine the Great initiates the rise to power of the Holy Roman Catholic Church. This brilliant political move by Constantine the Great helps fuse the empire and established the second major creed (first being the Apostles' Creed) known to this day as the *Nicene Creed* proclaiming the duality of Christ: 100% God / 100% man.

> *NICENE CREED (traditional wording)*
>
> *I believe in one God, the Father Almighty, maker of heaven and earth, and of all things visible and invisible; and in one Lord Jesus Christ, the only begotten Son of God, begotten of his Father before all worlds, God of God, Light of Light, very God of very God, begotten, not made, being of one substance with the Father; by whom all things were made; who for us men and for our salvation came down from heaven, and was incarnate by the Holy Ghost of the Virgin Mary, and was made man; and was crucified also for us under Pontius Pilate; he suffered and was*

---

[92] The first Christian council is found in Acts 15. It convened in Jerusalem to determine if new believers in Christ need to be circumcised. This second council is the first nationally recognized and sponsored council and was called together to debate Arianism and form a creed against this very influential heresy.

[93] The council of Nicea is the first council sponsored by a nationally recognized government.

> *buried; and the third day he rose again according to the Scriptures, and ascended into heaven, and sitteth on the right hand of the Father; and he shall come again, with glory, to judge both the quick and the dead; whose kingdom shall have no end.*
>
> *And I believe in the Holy Ghost the Lord, and Giver of Life, who proceedeth from the Father [and the Son]; who with the Father and the Son together is worshipped and glorified; who spake by the Prophets. And I believe one holy Catholic and Apostolic Church; I acknowledge one baptism for the remission of sins; and I look for the resurrection of the dead, and the life of the world to come. AMEN.*[94]

Although formally recognizing Christianity worked for Constantine's political ambitions, it did not go so well with the church, taking another one hundred years and two more major ecumenical councils to hammer out the concept of duality as it pertains to Jesus Christ and the Trinity.[95] Duality was officially recognized to exist by the leading brilliant minds of the early Church, and the *Nicene Creed* became the proclamation of faith recited by both Catholic and Protestant Churches around the world to this day, 1,700 years later.

Yet today's scientific community does not recognize duality when it is established outside of their paradigm. The idea of Jesus having a dual nature, 100% God / 100% man, is absurd to them and they dismiss the century of debates forging this major concept. Yet, the same community readily accepts duality when scientists declare duality. Articles on dualistic relationships in science are now common, *associating space with time,*

---

[94] <http://www.spurgeon.org/~phil/creeds/nicene.htm>
[95] Second nationally recognized ecumenical council was the Council of Constantinople (381 A.D.) and then the Council of Chalcedon (425 A.D.).

mass with energy, and particles with waves.[96] What this double-standard reveals is western culture's wholesale selling out to science. It just goes to show that idols aren't questioned as much as they are blindly followed, *i.e. worshipped.* It is like a blind person feeling the ear of an elephant concluding that elephants are thin and flexible, while another feels a leg declaring them thick and stiff. Cosmologists, are like these blind men, having no idea what it is they're getting into when it comes to "feeling out" God's vast Creation. Leading cosmologist, famous author, and internationally celebrated mathematician Stephen Hawking admits,

> *It appears that the fundamental numbers, and even the form, of the apparent laws of nature are not demanded by logic or physical principle.*[97]

The mind of God is far too deep for even the most gifted minds to wade into. God's Creation is beyond our comprehension. However, it should not keep us from striving to learn about our surroundings. While studying it, one should do so with humility and awe of our Great Creator. Something Hawking fails to do with his progressively bolder statements in each book he writes against a Creator of the universe,

> *...the multiverse concept can explain the fine-tuning of physical law without the need for a benevolent creator who made the universe for our benefit.*[98]

---

[96] Chappell, Dorothy, David E. Cook. *Not Just Science.* Zondervan: Grand Rapids, 2005. Print. (p.44)
[97] Hawking, Stephen, Mlodinow L. *The Grand Design.* Bantam Book: New York, 2010. Print. (p.143)
[98] Ibid. (p.165)

Quantum Physics

If Newton's classical physics is the birth of modern science, then the teenager would be Einstein's relativity physics and adulthood would then be quantum physics. And to quantum physics we must go. Quantum physics, ironically, provides amazing insights into some of our Lord's most perplexing biblical events—not that they need rationalizing—but when science provides us the opportunity to further understand biblical events, it would be irresponsible of us not to take the time to learn and grow from them. Then from here, later chapters in Part Three will tie this all together in a Christian Spaceview.

The paradoxical world of quantum physics began in 1900, with a hypothesis formed by German scientist Max Planck (1858–1947). Planck theorized that atoms release energy in specific packets or bundles called "Quanta."[99] One Quanta is the theorized smallest amount of energy in existence and released as an energy-wave instead of energy-particle. In separate work, Niels Bohr (1885–1962) determined that electrons orbit a nucleus at well-defined bands at fixed distances to the nucleus. Although today we know that electrons do not actually orbit in the traditional sense, they do remain within well-defined bands related to the level of energy each electron harbors. That is to say, the lower the energy level, the closer the band is to the nucleus.[100] On a side note, in order for an electron to drop to a lower band, it must shed energy. The energy shed is a photon, which is a particle-wave we see as light.

---

[99] Hawking, Stephen. *A Brief History of Time*. A Bantam Book: New York, 1996. Print. (p.55)

[100] Interestingly enough, particle physicists have confirmed the electron does not actually orbit a nucleus but vanishes then reappears in different locations within that band and so quickly, it gives the illusion of orbiting. Where it goes when it vanishes is still a mystery.

Then came German scientist, Werner Heisenberg (1901–1976), at the young age of 25, establishing the controversial, highly debated, even abhorred Heisenberg's Uncertainty Principle. It is this principle that establishes the cornerstone of quantum physics. This principle states that one cannot know both location and speed of an electron, only one or the other.[101] *Gone were the days of a clock-like universe...*[102] lamented many classical physicists. It seems God played a hand at the most basic foundational level of the cosmic order—uncertainty. Quantum mechanics was so disturbing even Einstein objected to it, declaring, *God does not play dice*, with Niels Bohr responding, *Stop telling God what to do.*[103] The ramifications of this principle in quantum physics, opens the door to help scientists see that Jesus controls physics. For centuries, skeptics have pointed at the miracles of Jesus revealed in Scripture as proof that the Bible is filled with myth and folklore, declaring the Bible as an unreliable source. Quantum physics, however, begs to differ. Let's consider a few examples.

Quantum Tunneling

With quantum physics came some pretty unnatural nature, such as quantum tunneling. This event occurs when an object does the impossible by physically passing through another object unscathed. For example, imagine you're on water skis and just cut out of the boat wake to line up with the ski jump fifty yards ahead of you and coming fast. The crowd watches in expectation as you clench your teeth, sharpen your focus, and grab the ski rope ever so tightly for the impact against the ramp—three feet, two, one, and

---

[101] As an electron sheds energy, it emits photons of light.
[102] Greene, Brian. *Elegant Universe*. Vintage Books: New York, 2000. (p.107)
[103] Kaku, Michio. *Parallel Worlds*. Doubleday: New York, 2005. Print. (p.160)

then…. no impact. Instead of feeling the familiar shock of your body mercilessly yanked up the ramp, you find yourself through the ramp, still skiing, completely unscathed, but on the other side of the ski ramp. Disoriented from the bewilderment of it all, you fall. Floating in the water, you look back at the ramp, over at your skis, and then take a quick assessment of yourself. Everything is as it should be. What just happened? You just went through the ramp. No cuts. No pain. No trapdoor in the ramp, and you just went right through it in the blink of an eye. The boat comes 'round with a wide-eyed skipper wondering what just happened. He picks you up and takes you to the ramp where you instinctively push against it, making sure it's there. Sure enough, you feel and hear the familiar "tunk" as you knock on it.

This seemingly impossible occurrence happens every single day. The most common form of quantum tunneling we know is called radiation. According to the laws of Newton's classical physics, radiation should not exist. It occurs when the nucleus of an atom, which is composed of protons and neutrons (in most cases) decays. Classical physics cannot account for how decay can radiate its energy through the nucleus since the nucleus is protected by a powerful sphere of energy known as the Strong Nuclear Force. Decay only employs the Weak Nuclear Force. The strong force might as well be a ten foot thick steel sphere surrounding the nucleus, yet a Geiger counter reveals radiation escaping the decaying nucleus constantly. This revealed that classical physics did not have all the answers to the workings of nature. Quantum physics, thanks to Neils Bohr's use of Heisenberg's Uncertainty Principle explains how this can be with quantum tunneling.[104]

---

[104] Hawking, Stephen. *A Brief History of Time, 10th Anniversary Edition*. A Bantam Book: New York, 2006. Print. (p.57)

Niels Bohr illustrated how by using the concept of "particles smeared out."[105] As they decay within the nucleus of an atom, the Weak Nuclear Force is given off and constantly fighting against its much bigger brother, the Strong Nuclear Force. The fight between them is relentless with radiation ricocheting back and forth within the nucleus at the speed of light, creating a virtual instantaneous presence within the nucleus at all times. This omnipresent-like state increases the probability of the Uncertainty Principle, allowing decaying particles to pass through the impenetrable barrier, since nothing is always for certain.

Even Einstein came around to embrace quantum mechanics, eventually receiving the Nobel Prize in Physics for his work in quantum theory. But then in his later years, as quantum theory progressively became more outlandish—physicist Richard Feynman's "Sum of All Histories" being a good example—Einstein became critical of it once again.[106] A biblical reality that quantum theory promotes, however, is the biblical idea that all things are possible.

Biblical Ramifications Of Quantum Tunneling

Read these accounts of Jesus after His resurrection from the dead:

> *On the evening of that first day of the week, when the disciples were together, with the **doors locked** for fear of the Jews, Jesus came and stood among them and said, "Peace be with you!" After he said this, he*

---

[105] Do not mistake this for individual particles all moving together to look like a wave. A particle is also a wave, simultaneously. Duality.
[106] Hawking, Stephen. *The Grand Design.* Bantam Book: New York, 2010. Print. (p.72)

> *showed them his hands and side. (John 20:19)* [bold mine]
>
> *While they were still talking about this, Jesus himself stood among them and said to them, "Peace be with you." They were startled and frightened, thinking they saw a ghost. He said to them, "Why are you troubled, and why do doubts rise in your minds? Look at my hands and my feet. It is I myself! Touch me and see; a ghost does not have flesh and bones, as you see I have. When he had said this, he showed them his hands and feet. (Luke 24:33–44)*

The disciples were huddled together behind a locked door, scared for their lives while mourning the loss of their Savior, when through that door walked Jesus. Notice that the author in this historic account didn't have Jesus stop at the door, pull out His keys and open it. Nor did he have Jesus knock on the door and wait for someone to unlock it and let Him in. Jesus physically walked through the locked door and says (and I love this part), "Shalom." This is a casual greeting equivalent to, "Hey, how are ya." I can't imagine the shocked thoughts that must have raced through their minds while probably all responding, "Good, how are You?" Jesus wasn't a phantom but physical. The scriptures are very careful to document this fact. How fitting for the Lord of Creation to employ quantum tunneling in His quantum physics. Yet the skeptics point to biblical accounts like this to diminish the Bible as mere folklore and myth. But now, even science has been forced to declare that the impossible is possible since duality exists and radiation exists. Christians might ask what took them so long? Thanks to the Uncertainty Principle and quantum tunneling, skeptics cannot just shrug off the stories of Jesus and His miracles as impossible and unreasonable—anything is possible, as quantum physicists calculates and the Creator of the Universe demonstrates.

Large Hadron Collider

With quantum physics comes new toys…er, tools, with the Large Hadron Collider (LHC) being the grandest. Scientist around the world agree the LHC has placed humankind on the brink of establishing a Grand Unified Theory of Everything. With the power-up of the LHC in Europe by the CERN group (European Organization for Nuclear Research) in September, 2008, physicists and mathematicians believe they can find the most fundamental particles present at the beginning of Creation. In so identifying these particles, they hope to realize Kepler's, Newton's, and Einstein's dream of one beautiful simple equation to unify and explain how the Universe works—from the unfathomably big to the incomprehensibly small. One grand unified explanation of everything.

The LHC represents an unprecedented global venture of 100+ countries, 10,000+ scientists and engineers costing the equivalent of 6 billion U.S. dollars.[107] The LHC is the largest particle accelerator, for that matter, the largest machine, ever built in human history. It is a circular laboratory seventeen miles in circumference buried five hundred and seventy feet below ground, crossing the borders of France and Switzerland. It requires ten thousand tons of liquid nitrogen and sixty tons of liquid helium in order to super-cool the entire seventeen mile laboratory for replicating deep space, which is near absolute zero.[108] In

---

[107] This is the U.S. equivalent. Actual amount was $4.6 Billion Swiss Francs.
[108] Deep Space is a balmy -454F (-271.3C), which on the Kelvin scale used by Cosmologist is only 1.9K.

these conditions, the LHC can accelerate particles and anti-particles to 99.99% the speed of light in opposing directions. They then collide to create the universe's most violent energy release known—so violent to even be controversial due to the ability to form mini black holes. Such power has created global concern among scientists, scholars, politicians, and outrage by citizens...this is the stuff of sci-fi, but it's real.

The LHC has now confirmed the existence of the elusive Higgs boson particle, which is theorized to be the source of all mass in all things. Imagine harnessing and manipulating mass itself. *For example: A car with no wheels hovering above a grass road. It can hover because a concentration of Higgs boson induced particles are focused above the car creating a well of gravity causing the car to "fall" up. And as you press the "gas pedal" another concentration of mass is focused in front of the car causing it to "fall" forward – moving effortlessly across town or to the moon and beyond.*

This behemoth "atom-smasher" will allow particle physicists to observe the smallest and most difficult particles and anti-particles in the universe. And this is of critical importance, since each theory must be tested to see if their theorized particles exist. The LHC will look for these particles, and if they are observed they will then know which theory has the most merit to continue pursuing.[109]

With such an equation of everything in hand, such a fundamental understanding of the relation of each cosmic force and their energies, scientists believe that humankind will be at the brink of a new era—an era manipulating and

---

[109] Greene, Brian. *The Elegant Universe.* Vintage Books: New York, 2000. Print. (p.10).

subduing the forces of nature itself. And it is one of these theories proposed, the most promising one, that we must now visit.

String Theory

String Theory was introduced in 1968 by Gabriele Veneziano and Mahiko Suzuki. It is in this year, when nuclear physicists first collided protons together at the Stanford Linear Accelerator, and to their dismay, countless unknown particles zoomed away at all angles:

> *...elementary particle physics was in total chaos, with atom smashers blasting nuclei apart...only to find hundreds more particles streaming out of the experiment.*[110]

The particles streaming out acted in unnatural, quirky ways. When you think of an explosion, you think of stuff flying away from the explosion on a reliable trajectory, but not with these particles. With each collision and violent explosion, they would zoom away, then stop and zoom back, then stop again and go in a different direction. It appeared that below the façade of natural order was chaos. The stuff that makes up atoms, was in chaos. All things—you, me, animals, plants, stars, planets, galaxies, etc.—are composed of chaotic particles moving in non-uniform motions and simultaneous directions. This was monumental in its discovery and in its ramifications. Veneziano and Suzuki developed String Theory to explain this strange new world of chaotic particles in a disarmingly simple and readily understandable way. But their theory squandered for two decades until the 1980s when Jon Schwarz of Cal Tech and Mike Green of Queen Mary

---

[110] Kaku, Michio. *Parallel Worlds*. Doubleday Books: New York, 2005. Print. (p.81).

College in London rediscovered it.[111] They modified the theory that has now become the crown jewel for hopefully explaining how to unify the cosmic forces into one grand force, a singularity that started it all—how Genesis 1 was done by God.

The mainstay beliefs set in stone by the Greeks two thousand years ago was that atoms were the smallest "things" in existence. J.J. Thomson, Ernest Rutherford, Niels Bohr, and James Chadwick shattered this long held belief by proving that even smaller particles exist within the atom: electrons, protons, and neutrons.[112] But instead of this ground-breaking discovery lasting another 2,000 years, it lasted just 38 years with the chaos of "sub-particles" crashing the proverbial party at Stanford. These sub-particles earned names like: quarks, charms, leptons, muons, bosons, up-quarks, down-quarks, charm-quarks, gluons, W bosons, Z bosons, Tauon, on and on and on, so much so that the famous, "J. Robert Oppenheimer joked that the Nobel Prize in physics *'should go to the physicist who did not discover a new particle that year.'*[113]

Instead of all these new countless and chaotic particles percolating under the surface of reality at the quanta level (also known as the Planck Scale), String Theory postulates that all these crazy particles are actually all the same thing: a string.[114] A string so incomprehensibly small that it does not exist in our four dimensional space-time but only within a one dimensional space at the quanta level, *...as small as a millimeter divided by a hundred-thousand-billion-billion-billion.*[115] In other words, they

---

[111] Ibid.
[112] Ibid (p.7)
[113] Ibid. (p.81)
[114] Ibid (p.7)
[115] Hawking, Stephen. *Universe in a Nutshell.* A Bantam Book: New

exist but don't exist as only a quantum entity can. At rest it is non-existent within our space-time realm, but should a quantum flux randomly and spontaneously occur, as Heisenberg's Uncertainty Principle allows, the string is disrupted from rest and vibrates causing ripples to appear in our space-time that we see as particles. The frequency of the vibration determines the energy of the particle and its characteristics. Since there are a myriad of frequencies at which a string can reverberate, there are then as many particles able to burst into physical existence for us to observe.

The ramifications of this theory are profound. Since LHC confirmed the presence of the elusive Higgs boson particle in 2013,[116] this makes String Theory and its derivative theories to be the most credible explanation of how our universe works. And the math explaining these theories requires the existence of six other spatial dimensions on top of our familiar four dimensions. This means ten total dimensions must exist. As God uttered Creation into existence, all these dimensions fought for prominence with God orchestrating the four we live in to win. The other six dimensions still exist but at the Planck scale of existence where they permeate every micro-millimeter of space across the universe—existing yet not existing.

A derivative of String Theory, known as M-Theory (with nobody in Cosmology able to explain what the "M" represents)[117] calculates that these other dimensions—

York, 2001. Print. (p.176)
[116] Interactions NewsWire #09-13, *The Higgs Boson: Past, Present, And Future*. February 18, 2013, Brookhaven National Laboratory. http:://www.interactions.org
[117] Hawking, Stephen, Mlodinow L. *The Grand Design*. Bantam Books: New York, 2010. Print.

together with the infinite number of particles and anti-particles that can exist—allow for billions and trillions of other universes to percolate out from the Creation event. Even now, our reality is just one of them. Remember this concept for future chapters of a Christian Spaceview.

Quantum physics and the Grand Unified Field Theory,[118] however, come at the expense of usefulness, as Hawking laments,

> ...*no matter how much information we obtain or how powerful our computing abilities, the outcomes of physical processes cannot be predicted with certainty because they are not determined with certainty. ...nature determines its future state through a process that is fundamentally uncertain.*[119]

And here is where faith exists. Whether one chooses science to believe in or Jesus Christ, it boils down to choosing which to believe. Do you choose modern science where randomness and uncertainty is its foundation every millisecond of every uncertain day; or in an ancient faith declaring a living God who created everything with a purpose. They are both fantastical, but only one is filled with miracles, hope, and purpose.

Heaven, Hell, And The LHC

Since the LHC team has confirmed the existence of Higgs boson as required in String Theory, then other dimensions and other universes are no longer just great plots in sci-fi movies, but legitimate and required for our space-time reality. Without realizing it, they are

---

[118] Ibid. (p.41)
[119] Ibid. (p.72)

legitimizing in scientific lingo the existence of other realities such as Heaven and Hell. For the first time in human history, science has legitimized such places as being real, physical, and not mere folklore, theological or mythological. However, you will probably not hear such things mentioned by scientists in the mainstream news, and even if a scientist did actually mention it, mainstream news would probably not post it or air it. Other dimensions or other universes, known as multiverse, should not be so disturbing to Christians since Heaven and Hell are part of our beliefs.

Regarding other dimensions or other universes, the Bible captures the accounts of Jesus fleshing out Heaven and Hell in language all people can understand. In the case of Heaven, He explains it as a real, physical place that we can breathe, eat, and sleep in:

> *In my Father's house are many rooms; if it were not so, I would have told you. I am going there to prepare a place for you. And if I go and prepare a place for you, I will come back and take you to be with me that you also may be where I am." (John 14:2-4).*

Some scholars argue that this account by Jesus is metaphorical. But, Jesus does not indicate it is nor do the writers who penned the account state it is figurative and the style of writing is not fiction. This scripture gives us a wealth of information about Heaven, indicating it is a place under construction to accommodate the human body. In order to do this, it must have at least three dimensions fabricated—height, width, and depth—in order for humans to survive. Furthermore, since Jesus said He is going there to *prepare*, this indicates not only is Jesus creating the physics for our Heaven but that it also requires time. Heaven then has at least four dimensions: height, width, depth, and time...but without the negative effects of time.

Scientist refer to these negative effects as entropy, *i.e. decay*. It is an actual observable, measurable, law of physics known as the Second Law of Thermodynamics. The Bible also refers to these negative effects as sin, which we associate with moral failure. Combine the scientific concept of entropy with the Biblical concept of sin, and you have an account for the physical[120] and spiritual[121] degradation of all things that I call, Sintropy. It seems, other dimensions are no longer reserved for sci-fi movies or mythological places in the Bible. The Bible and science both agree, for once, that Heaven and Hell can be real physical, touchable places as other dimensions or other universes.

Now that we have reviewed some profound conundrums in modern science such as duality, quantum tunneling, entropy, other dimensions, other universes, and their biblical parallels; we begin to catch a glimpse of God's creativeness as seen in His physics. I will now integrate these quantum concepts into the following chapters, beginning with the thought most people jump to when thinking about other Earths.

---

[120] Ontic. Material.
[121] Immaterial.

5. ARE WE ALONE?

Two possibilities exist: Either we are alone in the Universe or we are not. Both are equally terrifying.

~Arthur C. Clarke
(1917–2005)
Author/Futurist

On the cover of *National Geographic Magazine* an alien world basks in the warm glow of a yellow-orange Sun-like star. Written in bold letters, front-center, to help sell magazines hangs the age old question: "Are We Alone?"[122] Curiosity piqued, the reader looks down at the catchy subtitle: "Searching the Heavens for Another Earth." Hooked, they begin flipping through the pages in search of this feature story, and their search pays off with a full page feast of fire and light exploding out of a Delta II rocket piercing the night from Cape Canaveral, Florida. The roar is heard and the thunder felt as the Kepler payload shoots toward the heavens, illuminating Earth for miles around. Throngs of people on Cocoa Beach can be seen in the fierce glow staring up at the sudden rush of thunder and fire. And history will show this mission to be a key moment when, indeed, we begin to actually answer this age old question.

But, this pop-culture question is fatally flawed. When space became a race in '57 against the Russians, this question reached super-stardom across the globe, sparking our collective imagination. Twelve years and seventy-nine

---
[122] December 2009

Star Trek™ [123] episodes later with a young Captain Kirk, America took to the Moon on Apollo 11, winning the race to our closest cosmic neighbor. Then eight years later came *Star Wars*™ [124] advancing the frontiers of movie technology in 1977, making space travel look real and normal. It captured the imaginations of main-street America and became a pop-culture frenzy, inspiring the world to look to the stars. And look they did with Carl Sagan (1934-1996), a Pulitzer Prize winning Berkeley cosmologist hosting the popular PBS TV show *Cosmos*™. Debuting in 1980, it ultimately aired in over sixty countries and watched by an estimated five hundred million people.[125] Americans tuned in across the country soaking in every word he said and every star and planet explored with his famous line: *"Billions and Billions"* (heavily emphasizing the *"B"*). However, as much as I enjoy these movies and TV shows, the question, "Are We Alone?" implies no faith in a living God that cares for us and watches over us. At best, it might imply the deistic notion that if God exists, such a being no longer interacts in our universe. Cosmologist Stephen Hawking captures this mindset that many professors in universities across the country hold today:

> *These laws may have originally been decreed by God, but it appears that he has since left the universe to evolve according to them and does not now intervene in it.*[126, 127]

---

[123] Created by Gene Roddenberry, originally aired on CBS.
[124] Created and Directed by George Lucas under 20th Century Fox.
[125] Poundstone, William. *Carl Sagan: A Life In The Cosmos.* Holt Paperbacks: New York, 2000. Print.
[126] Hawking, Stephen. *A Brief History of Time.* A Bantam Book: New York, 1996. Print. (p.126)
[127] Theologians refer to this position as Deism, the belief in a God or Higher Power but that he, she, it, or they do not intervene in the affairs of the universe that "they" set in motion. Deism is not represented in the Bible, Theism is.

Such thinkers find this question, "Are We Alone?" perfectly legitimate. But it is illegitimate. In contrast to such a hopeless rumination, the Bible reveals again and again a clear answer to this question:

> *And Elisha prayed, "O LORD, open his eyes so he may see." Then the LORD opened the servant's eyes, and he looked and saw the hills full of horses and chariots of fire all around Elisha. (2 Kings 6:17)*

And not only is God with us, but Satan and his thugs are too:

> *The LORD said to Satan, "Where have you come from?" Satan answered the LORD, "From roaming through the earth and going back and forth in it." (Job 1:7)*

God and Satan are pursuing every human.

Again, we see the Lord proclaiming to the crowds, *He who has ears let them hear (Matthew 11:15)*. And Satan confides to those in earshot, *My name is Legion...for we are many (Mark 5:9)*.

Make no mistake…WE ARE NOT ALONE.

Skeptics Of Scripture

Since skeptics do not recognize scripture as a valid source for answering the question, "Are We Alone?" let's look to science, in many ways their religion, to see how clear of an answer it can provide.

Astrophysicists have calculated that the 400 billion stars orbiting the Milky Way are speeding around it at about 140 miles per second,[128] which is 139 miles per second faster than the average commercial jetliner. When astrophysicists simulate models of galaxies rotating at these speeds, it shows their stars flinging away like water off a Frisbee™. Apparently there is a missing a key ingredient in what keeps a galaxy together.[129] So they pursued this mystery with NASA's Cosmic Background Explorer (COBE) launched in 1989 and the Wilkinson Microwave Anisotropy Probe (WMAP) in 2001. Astronomers, physicists and mathematicians confirmed that the universe we currently see, measure, and study accounts for only 5% of the "stuff" that exists around all the galaxies across the universe holding them together.[130] Science cannot account for 95% of the "stuff" that makes up all things in the entire cosmos. And it is this stuff that keeps stars from flinging out of their own galaxies.

So what is keeping all the galaxies from flinging apart? Cosmologists are forced to conclude that something we can't see and are unable to measure must be in the "empty space" all around us throughout the universe. It seems space is not as empty as once thought.[131] Scientists have aptly called this missing stuff Dark Matter and Dark Energy. And this is a striking blow to skeptics (atheists, deists, and agnostics) and their need for evidence to prove things. An influential outspoken atheist said it this way:

> *...Bertrand Russell was once asked what he would say if, after dying, he were*

---

[128] Liddle, Andrew, Jon Loveday. *The Oxford Companion to Cosmology*. Oxford University Press: Oxford, 2008. Print. (p.203)
[129] Hawking, Stephen. *Universe in a Nutshell*. A Bantam Book: New York, 2001. Print. (p.184)
[130] Kaku, Michio. *Parallel Worlds*. Doubleday Books: New York, 2005. Print. (p.11)
[131] Actually, Greek philosophers and ancient astronomers believed "Aether" to be the element that fills the universe.

> *brought into the presence of God and asked why he had not been a believer. Russell's reply: "I'd say 'Not enough evidence God! Not enough evidence!'"*[132]

If evidence is their reason for believing in something, then they must conclude that our universe and our galaxies do not exist, for there is not enough evidence. Yet atheists and agnostics still cling to science in what to believe; staking their peace of mind and everlasting destiny on a mere 5% knowledge base. That is placing a tremendous amount of faith in a very small amount of information.

Missing: 95%

Our current technology for viewing the heavens relies solely on the electromagnetic field, where light exists. Scientist are blind to the "stuff" that makes up the bulk of material and energy in the universe since this so-called "Dark Matter" and "Dark Energy" do not utilize a light-based, electromagnetic, field. It utilizes something else.

The first indirect measurements verifying the existence of this mystery matter came from Maxim Markevitch and Doug Clowe in 2004. They compared images of a violent collision from the Chandra X-Ray Telescope against images from the Hubble Space Telescope. Peering deep into the universe, Markevitch and Clowe captured the violent fallout between two large galaxy clusters—not star clusters, but galaxy clusters—that had collided to form the Bullet Galaxy Cluster.[133] The stars

---

[132] Plantinga, Alvin. *Reason and Belief in God*. University of Notre Dame Press: Notre Dame, 1983. Print. (p.17–18)

[133] "*NASA Finds Direct Proof of Dark Matter.*" Release 06-297. Web.

seen by Hubble compared to the mass measured by Chandra revealed the bulk of the seeable stars is not where the bulk of its mass is. The stars are in one location and the mass is in another. The collision between all these galaxies sheared normal matter and dark matter apart. This became the first proof that stuff with a lot of mass exists and that we know nothing about it. Cosmologists now theorize that Dark Matter is what keeps stars from flinging out from their galaxies due to how heavy it is—far heavier than normal matter. Astrophysicists theorize that Dark Matter surrounds all galaxies to keep them together, or it is within galaxies making them much heavier than we can measure. So as far as skeptics go, using science to determine what to believe is an inadequate source.

Science Emphasizes My Insignificance

I remember the horror of once feeling lost as a kid. *Look at all that money!* my young mind of seven years screamed. The sparkling coins in the water caught my mind's eye as my family and I exited one of the exhibits at the Detroit Zoo. I was instantly mesmerized, *Wow! Take a look at this!* I gasped, while my mom and dad, older brother and two sisters kept on walking in the opposite direction. But I didn't notice. I remember standing there staring, marveling at all that money twinkling in the water, *There's gotta be hundreds of them!* I proclaimed with light reflections dancing in my eyes. *Oh, if I could only grab some!* I thought…and time no longer existed. *Man, all that money. There's gotta be hundreds of dollars in there! I think I can reach 'em with my hands too! I wonder if I would get in trouble…* raced my thoughts, while glancing at the other kids bewitched right along with me. But slowly, from deep within, a horror began to creep up in the back of

---

21 Aug. 2006. <http://www.NASA.gov./news.html>

my mind, realizing none of the voices around me sounded familiar. Looking around for my family, it hit me, I was all alone—nobody was there except a sea of strangers. Looking left then right, sheer panic captured me. All rationale ran away as my world collapsed in a moment. My body started trembling uncontrollably. Disoriented, I began walking blindly, screaming, *Mom! Dad!* I will never forget that feeling thirty-plus years ago—utterly lost, completely insignificant, alone.

To think a Being could look into our universe and find amongst billions of galaxies our average size galaxy, and within our 400 billion stars, an average yellow star, and then pinpoint a shadow of a small planet and hear my voice against billions of people, is rationally absurd. *Tilt* is all this "pinball machine" computes. Especially when these thoughts are reinforced by god-less singers, actors, authors and professors in the scientific community proclaiming that is absurd too. Their god-less interpretations of our space-time reality work to further devalue human significance; breeding a religion of hopelessness, futility, and feeling utterly alone. To clarify the term god-less, I do not mean evil people nor do I mean just atheists and agnostics, but all people who live life by their terms and their will alone. These people are living life less God, *i.e. God-less.* Evil and wicked people are actively against God, which means they acknowledge His existence and fight against Him. Evil and wicked people are not god-less but God-haters. Regarding the god-less within the scientific community, many years ago I bought a big picture book with marvelous images of the universe for my children to enjoy and learn from. One evening before their bedtime, they climbed upon my lap and I opened this big marvelous book. The two giant pages were all gray with small black lettering in the upper-left corner and the opening sentence shocked me as I read it in my mind: *In the beginning there was nothing.*[134] I remember feeling horrified inside and wondered what to do? I decided to simply grab the next page and start from there—the children never picked up on it. We looked at the pictures and read a few interesting pages then off too bed. After tucking them in and climbing aboard to pray with each of them, I left their rooms walking down the hall with the opening page of that book heavy on my mind. With some further thought and prayer, I decided to keep that big picture book in our story-collection shelf, thinking that someday, when my kids are older, it will allow for some great discussion—an opportunity to help my children develop critical-thinking skills. I envision them picking that book up on a summer day when they're bored out of their skulls and reading those words. And it is my hope that those words will ring troubling to them and that they will ask me about them. I can just picture the dialogue between me and one of my young "patawons"...

Dad? My son says with an inquisitive and confused tone.

Yes, Champ. I reply as I'm washing the dishes.

This science book says that in the beginning there was nothing.

I envision that I'll keep washing the dishes, acting unsurprised, and with a gentle tone that a wise sage on a mountaintop would be proud of, respond...*That is indeed what it says, Son. What do you think?*

I think they're wrong. He proclaims.

---

[134] Couper, Heather, N. Henbest. *Endless Universe.* Covent Garden Books: New York, 1999. Print.

But the answer will not completely satisfy me, as I want to know *why* he thinks they are wrong. So continuing my practiced fatherly look of profound wisdom, I'll then pause from my chores and turn to him, giving him my full attention, and ask him the six-hundred-thousand-dollar-question: *And why do you think they're wrong?*

And it is at this moment, I'll probably hold my breath while gazing upon my boy with serenity even the Dalai-Lama would be impressed with. But all the while, my mind will be racing through all the rearing and teaching and preaching over the years to bring us to this moment. He could give me many answers, but I have one golden answer in mind. One that I pray he'll say:

Because they have no proof.

And he is correct. That big picture-book mimicking a science book has no data, no measurable results, no proof that God did not exist before the universe. This children's picture book opens with a lesson on the author's god-less worldview. A worldview of futility and hopelessness, of being all alone and insignificant.

If this is how my son and daughter answer, it would tell me that my years of teaching them how to think critically has paid off—being able to recognize god-less worldviews cloaked as science. This will be a great day indeed. A day many adults have not yet reached, like the authors of that book.

Has science become so powerful in the minds of men and women that it seems to know no bounds; where even the beginning of time has now been given over to science for explanation. Is this because the human race has become so enlightened and wise? The answer becomes clear when one just looks at the wars and rumors of wars, poverty, disease, pollution, and vast spread of nuclear, biological, and chemical weapons across the globe. Humans are no more enlightened than any other generation, but more arrogant to think so.

Faith Emphasizes My Significance

Why did you close that book? Why didn't you say that prayer? Why did you close that book? Why didn't you say that prayer? Over and over it went around and around in my head. I couldn't focus, I couldn't think. The questions swirled, *Why did you close that book? Why didn't you say that prayer?* Slamming my calculus book shut, I yelled out, *Fine!* Just to make that annoying voice in my head stop. Pushing back my chair from my dorm room desk, I rummage through the trash to find that stupid little orange booklet, the title read, *Four Spiritual Laws*. It had been sitting on my dorm shelf for months and half-forgotten, until one day I got the inspiration to clean my dorm room. It was my freshman year studying for entry into the Aerospace Engineering College at Western Michigan University. I got the booklet from a stranger who handed it to me in a parking lot in front of Knauss Hall. I took it because she was wiggin' me out by handing me a religious booklet in public for others to see. I promised to read it and shoved the book in my pocket just to get her out of my hair. Months later, reading it in my dorm room, I dropped to my knees next to the warm glow of our banged up floor lamp and prayed this prayer in the booklet,

> *Lord Jesus, I need You. Thank You for dying on the cross for my sins. I open the door of my life and receive You as my Lord. Lead me and I will follow. Thank You for forgiving my sins and Your promise of everlasting life. I give You control. Make me the kind of person You want me to be.*[135]

And that stranger, Tina, became a good friend. That booklet showed me that I am not alone, that I matter to the Creator of the cosmos. God hears me when I speak and sees me when I look to Him. I am significant in a mind-numbingly huge universe. God reached into our space-time and intervened in my little life. I am so humbled and grateful and dumbfounded by such love.

It is just another deep confirmation that our flaws do not stop God. In His grace and mercy, he upsets the natural order of things on a daily basis through the supernatural work of His Holy Spirit.[136] His Spirit intervenes in our lives. Such intervention is proof to those who have experienced it that we are significant. That we are not alone.

Ahhh, peace and quiet, I muse, wrapping myself in a blanket while settling down into my favorite rocker on our deck. *The kids are off to their slumber parties, and my beautiful bride left for a night with the girls*, my mind reviews. The bonfire warms my cheeks and nose as I draw a long sip of hot apple cider and spiced rum. A smile spreads across my face. The Sun is proving its reliability once again with God's artwork unfolding before my eyes—to the left I see a darkening purple sky, while up above me,

---

[135] Bright, Bill. *Four Spiritual Laws*. Campus Crusade for Christ: San Bernardino, 1965. Print.
[136] a priori

deep-blue, climaxing into a brilliant orange-red sunset to the west. The birds, crickets, and frogs cheer the Artist as the fiery chariot finishes its spectacular race across the sky once again. The view and colors and symphony of sounds combined with cool crisp air heighten my senses, causing my soul to leap within me bringing to mind the words of a song:

> *Blessed be Your name*
> *When the sun's shining down on me*
> *When the world's 'all as it should be'*
> *Blessed be Your name*[137]

God's Spirit confirms within my soul the magnificence of our Great Creator through His Creation,[138] even this broken one. St. Augustine said it well when he declared fifteen hundred years ago, while the light from a hundred-thousand-plus stars were only half-way through the relentless journey to Earth: *Some people read books in order to find God. Yet there is a great book, the very appearance of created things. Look above you! Look below you!*[139] This ancient testament Augustine refers to is proclaiming that we are not alone. Science and Astronomy have done well at exploring God's Creation and providing answers to its many wonders, but poorly at interpreting the findings. More on this later. What if astronomers and cosmologists and astrophysicists and the professors in the universities responded to each scientific discovery, such as other Earths with praise to God: *Praise him, sun and moon, praise him, all you shining stars. (Psalm 148:3).*

---

[137] "Blessed Be Your Name" written by Matt Redman. Copyright 2005.
[138] Do not mistake this for Natural Theology. It is only through God's special revelation captured in the pages of the Bible that one can realize salvation.
[139] Chappell, Dorothy F., E. David Cook. *Not Just Science.* Zondervan: Grand Rapids, 2005. Print. (p.30)

Instead of the god-less asking, "Are we alone?" to which the answer is a resounding, "No!" A more accurate question would be: Is there other intelligent life in our universe?

6. ALIEN LIFE

If we long to believe that the stars rise and set for us, that we are the reason there is a Universe, does science do us a disservice in deflating our conceits?

~Carl Sagan
(1934–1996)
Astronomer/Author

NASA launches a $200 million space probe on a risky expedition into the Asteroid Belt, not only to take images of comet Wild 2, but to actually plunge into its heart and capture a sample. Five years pass, and at long last a command is given to bring the spacecraft aptly named Stardust to life. Stardust powers up, checks its systems and begins closing in on the brilliant comet. If you were sitting at the helm of Stardust, you would see the spectacular shimmering tail trailing off to the right, away from the Sun, and extending out over a thousand miles. It would make you feel like a speck of dust. Stardust is indeed the perfect name, for it is but a speck of dust in comparison to the comet that spans the width of the United States from Michigan to Florida. NASA adjusts the craft's trajectory away from the tail in order to invade the turbulent coma at the head of the comet. Before making history, Stardust receives a command to open a hatch exposing a collector plate the size of a tennis racquet coated with a special silica-based gel.[140] The gel is designed to capture the frozen material spewing out of the asteroid on its race toward our

---

[140] Trademarked as *Aerogel*, which is 99% air, this gel has been used by NASA for decades.

Sun. NASA then executes a command mankind has never ventured before. Not only is it dangerous enough to enter into the Asteroid Belt, but to leave the vacuum of space, creeping into an alien atmosphere filled with eons of mystery. Ever so slowly, Stardust wanders through the coma's haze with NASA hoping to capture the stuff of folklore. Upon several successful passes dipping in and back out of the Comet's head over the course of several hours, the collector plate is told to retract and seal itself for the long trip home. Two years later, Stardust rendezvous with Earth and releases the capsule holding the plate with Wild 2 inside. Re-entering Earth's atmosphere, it parachutes down to a soft landing at the U.S. Air Force Test Range in Utah on January 15, 2006. What it holds inside will prove well worth the seven year round trip.

Why sample the stuff of a comet? A comet is a rogue asteroid that was yanked out of its random orbit from one of three asteroid belts in our solar system. The closest asteroid belt is named just that, Asteroid Belt, and lies between Mars and Jupiter where the dwarf planet Ceres lingers. Another belt is beyond Uranus called the Kuiper Belt where dwarf planet Pluto resides, and the final field is at the outer-edge of our solar system named the Oort Cloud, which is a full light-year from the Sun.[141] As an asteroid breaks from its ancient orbit, the Sun's gravity draws it inward causing it to warm up and pick up speed. A comet is no more than a thawing asteroid.

Like a wide-eyed child seeing fireworks blaze across the night for the first time, comets used to be considered ominous signs among civilizations around the world. For most of mankind's existence, they were treated

---

[141] To give you an idea of distance, the two Voyager spacecrafts launched in the 1970s are speeding along at 35,000 mph, and will take about 40,000 years to reach the Oort Cloud.

as signs of great change on the horizon. Kings feared them; witch doctors, false prophets and astrologers profited from them; and the whole world wondered what these glorious objects could be. The Stardust Mission not only dared to approach such a mystical object, but employed cold scientific precision to trespass within it and capture the stuff of lore, the stuff that has inspired thousands of years of human civilizations. These mysterious beacons racing across the night sky are perfectly preserved, frozen in time, since God uttered His famous words, *Let there be...*[142] As for what they found in Stardust's collector plate, it proved worth the hundreds of millions of dollars spent. Stardust principal investigators at the Johnson Space Center, using an electron microscope, scoured the *aerogel,* finding fascinating and alien minerals—but one item stood out. They identified within the gel an amino acid, specifically, Glycine. Geneticists have shown that Glycine is a key ingredient for the building of protein, which in turn, is one of the building blocks of DNA—the nucleic acid carrying the genetic code for every form of living thing.[143]

NASA Discovers A Young Universe

This discovery reveals two important details about Creation: First, that the elements critical for life were there at the beginning.[144] Evolutionary cosmologists purport that

---

[142] Genesis 1 reveals that creation only took seven days. However, cosmologists present evidence that our star, the Sun, is a third or fourth generation star from when time began billions of years ago. My chapter Ten presents the case that they are both right and how.
[143] Steigerwald, Bill. *Goddard Spaceflight Center.* 17 Aug. 2009. Web. <http://www.nasa.gov/centers/goddard/home/index.html>. Note: Geologists also discovered Amino Acids in a carbon-rich (carbonaceous chondrite) meteor that struck Australia in 1969 known as the Murchison meteor (many like this have been found since). However, this is the first time it has been captured in space, where it is assured not to be contaminated from contact with Earth's atmosphere.

the ingredients of life as we know it slowly evolved by trial and error and chance over a 13.7 billion year span of time. This span of time is the theorized existence of the cosmos, which includes the final four hundred million years of our solar system's evolution.[145] Yet, here it is, evidence frozen in time showing that a critical building block of life as we know it was there at the beginning. Cosmologists would proclaim, yes, at the beginning of our solar system. But when I say beginning, I am referring to the Genesis account of the beginning. Chapter Ten will show how this can be, how NASA captured nothing less than material from the original Genesis event. Evidence of a key ingredient of life was at the beginning. It did not evolve by trial and error and chance over billions of years.

Second and finally, it further validates that the universe we see has a purpose. That our solar system, our galaxy, and the web of galaxies across our seeable universe are well suited for life since the beginning. Carl Pilcher, director of the NASA Astrobiology Institute, puts it this way:

> *The discovery of Glycine in a comet supports the idea that the fundamental building blocks of life are prevalent in space, and strengthens the argument that life in the Universe may be common rather than rare.*[146]

---

[144] What goes along with Instant Creation is an idea known as Spontaneous Generation, whereby life spontaneously occurred. Bertrand Russell, as well as many biologists, holds to the opposing view known as biological determinism. This view believes life evolved from the universe via natural causes taking billions of years before the first living cell even appeared 3,800 million years ago.
[145] This is the current in vogue estimate by cosmologists.
[146] Henderson, Mark. "Discovery by Stardust probe in Wild 2 comet suggests life on Earth began in space." *Times Online.* Web. 19 Aug.

On Earth, many scientists have documented just how abundant and robust life can be. They show it thriving in seemingly inhospitable places that give further argument that life is not fragile but tenacious, capable to survive in the most extreme environments. For example, along the Asian Pacific Rim within the Mariana Trench, a modified submarine named *Trieste* (1960) descended for four hours to reach the very bottom of the planet, where the entire weight of the ocean presses 1,099 times that of sea-level. Upon touch down, they turned on their lights and discovered living organisms thriving on life-giving minerals spewing from super-heated vents courtesy of the Earth's molten mantle. Scientists have also found life in the coldest place on Earth, Antarctica, where temperatures plunge to -129 degrees Fahrenheit. Life on this planet thrives in the sunshine or total darkness, with air or no air, with heat or freezing cold—life abounds. This idea that our planet seems ideal for life is known among cosmologists as the Anthropic Principle.

Anthropic Principle

This principle was formed by scientists whom studied the heavens and began to see how ideal it appears to be for life. One might call it a god-less Genesis story. Stephen Hawking contemplates it this way:

> *If the rate of expansion one second after the big bang had been smaller by even one part in a hundred thousand million, [the universe] would have re-collapsed before it reached its present size. ...the odds against a universe like ours emerging out of something like the big bang are enormous. I*

2009. < http://www.timesonline.com>

> *think there are clearly religious implications.*[147]

Hawking's honesty is deeply appreciated here, though it lacks sincerity as seen in his most recent book that so adamantly argues against such implications.[148] Nevertheless, Hawking is simply revealing how staring into the heavens moves all people to ponder deep things that go way beyond science. As the Bible proclaims:

> *For what can be known about God is plain to them, because God has shown it to them. Ever since the creation of the world his eternal power and divine nature, invisible though they are, have been understood and seen through the things he has made. (Romans 1:19–20)*

Theologians have known of this quality about Creation for centuries, calling it the *Teleological Argument.*[149] This paradigm recognizes the abundance of life, tenacity of life, and most importantly, the seemingly ideal design of our universe to harbor life. When one factors these truths into the billions of galaxies existing across our local universe, it builds a reasonable case toward other life existing somewhere within our seeable cul-de-sac of space. NASA believes this so strongly that they have already awarded Northrop Grumman a contract for fabrication of the James Webb Space Telescope.[150] This gold-plated telescope is $2.5+ billion in the making, and set for a 2018

---

[147] Kaku, Michio. *Parallel Worlds.* Doubleday Books: New York, 2005. Print. (p.348)

[148] *The Grand Design,* published by Bantam Books in 2010 is his latest book, but not just on physics but meta-physics as well I would say.

[149] Also known as *Analogy of Being.*

[150] James Webb Space Telescope has been named the successor to the aging Hubble Space Telescope.

launch. One of its ambitious missions is to scour Kepler's new found habitable worlds for signatures of life. I would tend to dismiss such a mission as sci-fi, but it seems we have entered a new age in this new millennium, where questions that have been pondered throughout human history can now be answered.

This new telescope hosts a 260-inch-diameter (6.6 Meter) mirror, almost three times the light gathering power of Hubble's 94-inch-diameter mirror. James Webb's specialty will be spectral analysis. This time-proven science was discussed in chapter one.

It will study these habitable worlds as they eclipse their "Sun." during the eclipse, some of the star's light will pass through the atmosphere of the planet. Some of the light waves from the star will be absorbed by specific gases in the atmosphere leaving a black space within the rainbow of colors that star produces in spectral analysis. These blank spaces in the rainbow reveal which specific gases exist in the planet's atmosphere. For example, our sky is blue because all the other colors from our Sun get absorbed by all the other gases. This is also the general reason why Mars's sky looks pink. It is also the same reason why the video footage seen from the Huygens' probe, as it parachuted through the atmosphere of Saturn's moon Titan, looks yellowish brown.[151] It is these absorption lines that NASA plans to use to determine which planets have atmospheres similar to Earth's.

Of the gases in those atmospheres, the one that will prove most exciting is not oxygen. NASA will be searching these alien atmospheres for telltale signs of methane. Methane breaks down over time requiring constant

---

[151] January 14, 2005, Cassini spacecraft released the Huygens probe, successfully touching down on Saturn's moon Titan.

replenishment. Biological life processes are what replenish it. For example: The Environmental Protection Agency (EPA) has estimated that cows squeeze out as much as eighty million metric tons of methane annually on our own aromatic planet.[152] Methane is a telltale sign of life.

Having promoted the idea that alien life seems likely by presenting the cosmologist's perspective, I must temper this with modern biology's pessimistic outlook on such life. Many molecular biologists agree with Paul Agutter when he bluntly states,

> ...*the probability that multicellular organisms exist anywhere else in the universe is not very high...*[153]

This is a good, sobering statement when discussing other life in the universe. It should remind us that cosmologists, astrophysicists, mathematicians, and astronomers are not qualified to make such conclusions on life. It would be the same as a five-star chef making conclusions on the design of a NASCAR™ race engine—they are untrained to do so, but still might if they are arrogant enough to think they can. No matter how brilliant the cosmologist (which are typically physicists and mathematicians), they are only qualified in the search for other planets—not whether life exists there. The debates and discussions on other life are more appropriate within other disciplines, namely, biology and theology. Biology, since the biologist can speak on the physical needs of carbon-based life as we know it; and theology, since the theologian can speak on the metaphysical nature that makes life intelligent. That is to say, theologians champion the

---

[152] Google: "EPA livestock methane emissions"
[153] Agutter, Paul S., Denys N. Wheatley. *About Life Concepts in Modern Biology*. Springer: Netherlands, 2007. Print. (p.118)

immaterial aspects of life while biologists champion the material aspects; two sides of the same coin.

Categories Of Life As We Know It

An artist doesn't create just one poem or just one painting or just one sculpture. No, an artist creates again and again and again because it is their passion; it is what they do. As the Apostle Paul, who wrote two-thirds of the New Testament, reveals, one way to think of God is to imagine a Master Artist:

> ...Shall what is formed say to him who formed it, 'Why did you make me like this?' Does not the potter have the right to make out of the same lump of clay some pottery for noble purposes and some for common use? (Romans 9:20–21)

As a Master Artist, God forms things, lots of things, and for reasons only He knows. I've often wondered what God did after the seventh day of Creation. Did God stop creating? Has God been twiddling His "thumbs" for all eternity since? How about before the first day of Creation? What did God do for all eternity past? It does not seem unreasonable for God to speak countless worlds and alien life into existence (known as Multiverse), for God is the God of all eternity past and all of eternity future. It is humbling to think about.

As for the word "life," do we mean a single-celled form of life or something more complex, like plant life, or even more complex, like animal life, or exponentially and incomprehensibly more complex, like human life?

Determining what kind of life something is, is a discipline within biology known as taxonomy. This area of study dates back to the era of Classical Greece more than two thousand years ago. Modern taxonomy began with Carl Linnaeus (1707–1778) listing several thousand species under two basic kingdoms: the plant kingdom and the animal kingdom. He broke the animal kingdom further into vertebrate, which entailed all mammals, birds, reptiles, amphibians, and fish, and then all other forms of animal life into invertebrates. In the case of humans, we were categorized as vertebrates under the animal kingdom. For more than two hundred and fifty years this classification system reigned.[154] But, as they discovered more and more living organisms, this simpler classification system began to break down. Biologists now recognize Earth to hold as many as one hundred million different forms of life.[155] To keep up, a third kingdom titled, Monera, was added in the 19th century representing all microscopic organisms.[156] And since then, two more kingdoms have been added giving us five kingdoms in taxonomy today.[157] For example:

> Kingdom: Animal
> Phylum: Chordates
> Order: Mammals
> Class: Primates
> Family: Hominids
> Genus: Homo
> Species: Sapiens[158]

Notice how modern biology reveals their god-less worldview by refusing to recognize the immaterial/spiritual nature of humans. Emil Brunner, one of the greatest theologians of the twentieth century, put it this way:

---

[154] Ibid.
[155] Ibid. (p.119)
[156] Ibid.
[157] Ibid.
[158] Ibid.

> *Man must first of all be defined theologically; only then may the philosopher, the psychologist and the biologist make their statements.*[159]

The Bible sings it this way,

> *I praise you because I am fearfully and wonderfully made. (Psalm 119:14)*

Instead, modern biology lumps us into the same kingdom as rats.

Let us correctly review the categories of life recognizing the meta-physical/immaterial nature intertwined within humans.

The Bible's account of life captures two vital spiritual properties that must be understood and properly categorized. To critique these key properties, I will breakdown the Genesis account of living things into three common categories used among theologians, though the titles among theologians may vary. These three general categories are:

Lower Life Forms:
- Microbial life: amoebas, plankton, bacteria, fungi, protists, etc…
- Plant life: flowers, trees, moss, seaweed, shrubs, vegetables, etc…
- Fish

Higher Life Forms:

---

[159] Brunner, Emil. *Man in Revolt: A Christian Anthropology.* 1957. The Lutterworth Press: Cambridge, 2002. Reprint

- Animal life: mammals, birds, reptiles, amphibians, bugs, mollusks, etc...

Imago-Dei Life Forms:
- Self-aware, self-determined, conscious beings able to create cultures. Cultures include the development of complex civilizations practicing the arts, academics, and religion. Humans.

Lower Life Forms

To understand these three forms of life, let's look at Genesis chapter one and chapter seven:

> *Then God said, "I give you every seed-bearing plant on the face of the whole earth and every tree that has fruit with seed in it. They will be yours for food. And to all the beasts of the earth and all the birds of the air and all the creatures that move on the ground—everything that has the **breath of life** in it—I give every green plant for food." And it was so. (Gen 1:29–30)[bold mine]*

> *They had with them every wild animal according to its kind, all livestock according to their kinds, every creature that moves along the ground according to its kind and every bird according to its kind, everything with wings. Pairs of all creatures that have the **breath of life** in them came to Noah and entered the ark. The animals going in were male and female of every living thing, as God had commanded Noah.*

> *Then the LORD shut him in. (Gen 7:14–16)[bold mine]*

Those forms of life void of God's *breath of life* are categorized as lower life forms.[160] Discussing the possibility of lower life forms on alien worlds is, dare I say, the easy part. As Kepler flags potential planets, NASA's international co-op of ground-based telescopes will further analyze them to confirm how many planets and what size, density, and distance they are from their star. And most importantly, which of them orbit within their star's habitable zone. Since lower life forms do not require this immaterial property referred to as the *breath of life*, theology, then, does not have to be a variable in the equations for lower life forms to exist on these worlds. Therefore, in the case of lower life forms, scientific equations will properly direct NASA to habitable worlds that could very well harbor such simple life. That is to say, one plus one does equal two. If there is liquid water, then lower life forms as we know them may exist there. Molecular biologists, however, would still disagree. They would say it is not as easy as one plus one. They state that the number of biological systems involved to form any kind of life is statistically rare and improbable within an evolutionary cosmology.[161] Even so, in light of the hundred billion galaxies estimated to exist just in our seeable universe and the number of stars in each of those galaxies, improbable becomes probable. Lower life forms, then, are probable. But, when it comes to higher life forms their equations will not add up. Such discussions must carry an

---

[160] A more in depth discussion on the original Hebrew word used for 'breath of life' is found under the discussion of higher life forms.
[161] Russell, Robert J., Nancy Murphy, C.J. Isham. *Quantum Cosmology and the Laws of Nature: Scientific Perspectives on Divine Action.* 2nd Ed. Vatican Observatory Publications: Vatican City State; The Center for Theology and the Natural Sciences: Berkeley. 1996. Print.

additional variable that transcends biology, math, and physics. Where we must travel now is into the supernatural, where the immaterial originates. For this discussion, scientists will need to shut down their supercomputers, walk away from their mighty telescopes, power down their atom-smashers, and enter into a discipline much older. All further discussions on higher life forms and beyond will require the wisdom of ancient men from a time scientists mock and call the Dark Ages and from a book they attempt to mock even more.

Higher Life Forms

The Holy Bible reveals a progression in the book of Genesis from lower life forms to higher life forms, climaxing in the creation of self-aware, self-determined, conscious life forms.[162] But some say such an interpretation of Genesis one and two is too literal, too fundamental; since Genesis is not a first-hand account. Genesis tells of events that occurred before writing even existed. This is true. Western culture owes its ability to read and write to the Phoenicians (c. 1050 B.C.). It is their alphabet that Old Hebrew, the language of the Old Testament, is derived from. It is also their alphabet that gave birth to Greek, the language of the New Testament; Latin, the language of the Roman Empire; and English, the most common language in all of human history. So, taking the Genesis account of Creation as exact historical fact, when the written word did not yet exist, causes many scholars to downgrade Genesis as merely good stories for children. But, there was a first-hand witness who patiently waited for humans to invent writing. Theologians across all traditional Christian denominations agree that the third person of the Trinity was there on the day of Creation and patiently waited for

---

[162] Reymond, Russell. *A New Systematic Theology of Christian Faith.* Thomas Nelson Publishers: Nashville, 1998. Print. (p.416)

humans to develop words in order to guide their pens.[163] The scribes must have marveled at what they wrote and did not fully understand all that they wrote.[164] Time passed, prophecies were fulfilled, and we now enjoy the fuller meaning of the ancient texts that they could only hold in wonder and awe. Theologians refer to this effect as *Sensus Plenior* (sense-us-plen-oor), which is Latin for, *the fuller sense*.

I hold out for the inspiration of scripture, not as a literalist nor as a fundamentalist, but as one who has been changed by that same Spirit. I am a first-hand witness to the existence of the Spirit of God. I did not change me, but when I laid down my will and chose to follow Christ's will, it is then that the Word of God became alive to me. My soul was reignited by God's Spirit that now dwells within me. I remember that evening in my college dorm room, the verses moved me deeply, shouting to me within my mind so loudly that I found myself responding out loud in order to hear my counter-arguments against this undeniable calling. To this day, the words within the Bible resonate within me. It resonates beyond the material properties of me and into the immaterial properties of me, where deep calls to deep. All followers of Jesus Christ have had this experience.[165] If you find yourself wondering about it, the fact that you are reading this book is a sign that God is indeed calling you. Dig deeper by reading the gospel of

---

[163] 2 Timothy 3:16 is a good place to start for a study on this concept of the inspiration of scripture.

[164] Although Moses is held as the traditional author of Genesis, bible scholars and literary critics highlight stylistic differences throughout the text indicating scribes under him may have assisted. For more information see the *Word Biblical Commentary*: Genesis 1–15 by Gordon J. Wehnham: *The Book of Genesis*: Chapters 1–17 by Victor P. Hamilton.

[165] "Disciples" is the biblical term for those who follow Jesus Christ.

John chapter 3 and the book of Romans chapters 3, 6, and 10 to discover the fuller meaning you were intended for.

So I am approaching the Genesis account of Creation as a truth that humans aren't fully capable of understanding, like quantum tunneling or the duality of electrons. Humans understand the account of Creation enough to know there is a fuller meaning in it. We see a glimpse into Genesis one's *Sensus Plenoir* where the Bible introduces a new mysterious term: $n^e samah^{166}$ (ne-shah-mah) meaning, "breath of life":

> *And to all the beasts of the earth and all the birds of the air and all the creatures that move on the ground—everything that has the breath of life in it... (Genesis 1:29–30)*

Most linguists around the world translate this word into either "breath of life" or "soul" in the many occurrences found in Scripture. Higher life forms, such as birds and animals, were gifted with God's $n^e samah$. An excellent illustration of God's special concern for higher life forms is in the account of Noah's flood:

> *And rain fell on the earth forty days and forty nights. On that very day Noah and his sons, Shem, Ham and Japheth, together with his wife and the wives of his three sons, entered the ark. They had with them every wild animal according to its kind, all livestock according to their kinds, every*

---

[166] There are multiple spellings of this word: *Strong's Exhaustive Concordance*: "neshamah," *Vine's Expository*: "nepesh." Reymond's spelling from his work, *A New Systematic Theology of the Christian Faith*, was used.

> *creature that moves along the ground according to its kind and every bird according to its kind, everything with wings. Pairs of all creatures that have the <u>breath of life</u> in them came to Noah and entered the ark. (Genesis 7:12–16) [underline mine]*

What form of life did not enter the ark? Plants and fish. Fish for obvious reasons, but it appears that God was less concerned with lower life forms than with higher life forms. Animals were cared for, showing to be of a greater concern to God, perhaps due to this added variable in their equation for life. Sure, God directed Adam and Eve to care for the garden, indicating God has concern for plant life, but nowhere in Scripture does it indicate any vegetation received the *breath of life* by God.

So why go into all this? Because it has universal implications that can be transferred to *all* possible higher forms of life no matter the planet. An animal lives only after God breathes upon it, regardless of how habitable the planet. It is a transcendent variable that science cannot measure. Therefore, to the frustration of exo-biologists, one plus one does not equal two when it comes to animal life…no matter the planet. God's *breath of life* is an uncertainty principle in the science of higher life forms. Since the uncertainty principle is now recognized within modern science, today's scientists cannot just brush aside the immaterial aspects of higher life forms simply because they cannot be measured.

Although this wild card, *n^{e}samah*, can only be played by God, humans still hold an ace with the Kepler Spacecraft and future James Webb Space Telescope. Mankind will soon be able to spectrally analyze the atmospheres of these habitable worlds in search of God's wild card. If NASA discovers other life, just what category of life will it be?

7. INTELLIGENT ALIEN LIFE

On Earth, among millions of lineages of organisms and perhaps 50 billion speciation events, only one led to high intelligence; this makes me believe its utter improbability.

~ Ernst Mayr
(1904–2005)
Biologist/Taxonomist

When it comes to intelligent life, our ponderings must delve deeper in, beyond the discussion of nature, beyond the subject of souls, and transcend into the eternal—into the profound.

I must say, I hesitate at delving into this because frankly, nobody, not scientists, philosophers, or theologians, can fully grasp nor completely define what intelligent life is. It simply transcends what God's creatures can fathom. But, what I can do is at least point us in the right direction and provide a glimpse that tends to rub modern scientists the wrong way. The direction we must take is back to the beginning:

> *Then God said, "Let us make man in our image, in our likeness, and let them rule over the fish of the sea and the birds of the air, over the livestock, over all the earth, and over all the creatures that move along the ground." So God created man in his own image, in the image of God he created him;*

male and female he created them. (Genesis 1:26–28)

Humans alone are made in the image of God; all other life forms on this planet are not. This metaphysical property places you, me, all of humanity, a quantum leap above and beyond the plant and animal kingdoms that make up the lower and higher life forms discussed in the previous chapter. Yet, biology's god-less, positivistic worldview refuses to recognize this critical property that exists (yet doesn't exist) within men and women. Without it, we would just be really smart animals, like monkeys or dolphins for example. Being in God's *image and likeness* is so foundational to who we are as humans, that it is introduced in the very first chapter of the Bible. Like a teacher who must first introduce numbers and how to count before teaching addition and subtraction, God here is doing the same in Genesis one on the discussion of intelligent life. The most common term used among Bible scholars today when referring to this holy human property is *imago Dei* (eh-ma-go-day-ee). *Imago Dei* is a term born out of Latin, the language of the Roman Empire. Latin outlived the mighty empire remaining the choice of scholars throughout western civilization for over a thousand years. Copernicus wrote his revolutionary book in Latin and so did Kepler. *Imago Dei* is found in the Vulgate, the Latin translation of the Bible written by the great scholar Jerome (347 A.D.–420 A.D.). His translation is known as the King James Version. The literal Latin translation for *imago* means "image of" and *Dei* means "God." The most brilliant scholars of Christendom have debated and developed this mysterious revelation in Genesis for countless generations. All the while, photons from one hundred thousand plus stars in the Northern Cross carry on their epic journey to our small blue dot. Over these ages, western theologians have come to understand that human life would not be actualized, conscious, moral creatures without *imago Dei.* We must first glimpse a small understanding of what it is and then how this immaterial nature plays such a critical role in the discussion of intelligent life—no matter the planet.

Scholars have drawn three general views on what it means to be in God's *imago Dei:* Substantive View, Relational View, and Functional View.[167]

The Substantive View is the idea that we are the physical and psychological images or reflections of God Almighty. Jesus is the ultimate proof of this since He is in the image of the son of man (human) and the son of God. The Relational View is western theology's most popular view championed by St. Augustine (354 A.D.–430 A.D.) who explained that exploring the mysterious idea of *imago Dei* starts with understanding the relationship of the Trinity: "The Father is the lover, the son the beloved, and the spirit the love that is between them and that unites them."[168] This view was also championed by Karl Barth (1886–1968) and Emil Brunner (1889–1966) in the 20th century, arguing that as we practice harmony within our relationship to God, within our relationship to our self, and within our relationship to others, we reflect the image of God, *i.e. imago Dei*. And finally, the most interesting and appropriate view to aid our discussion on intelligent alien life is the Functional View. This has gained much popularity due to its attention to caring for the environment. This view, too, has enjoyed a long history and promotes the *image and likeness* of God by what we do:

---

[167] Ericson, Millard. *Christian Theology.* 2nd Ed. 1983. Baker Books: Grand Rapids, 2000. Print.
[168] Smail, T. *Like Father Like Son.* William B. Eerdmans Publishing: Grand Rapids, 2006. Print. (p.75). As quoted from St. Augustine's fifteen volume work, *De Trinitate,* written between 400 – 416 AD.

> *God blessed them and said to them, 'Be fruitful and increase in number; fill the earth and **subdue** it. **Rule** over the fish of the sea and the birds of the air and over every living creature that moves on the ground. (Genesis 1:27–28) [bold mine]*

God commands humans to *subdue*, meaning: oversee, care for, and manage the Earth. If we fail to take care of our planet, we fail to reflect the *image and likeness* of God. It goes even further in that it also establishes what actions we should pursue in our personal lives:

> *...to mirror in our humanity the initiation of the Father [leadership], the obedience of the Son [loyalty], and the creativity of the Spirit [the arts: music, dance, painting] as the harmonious but distinct expressions of the free love of God within a human life and human community....* [169]

It is this *imago Dei* gift that defines the secret to having meaning, purpose, and fulfillment in our own life. It is also the sole criteria separating humans from all lower and higher life forms. To be an intelligent life form is to possess the gift of *imago Dei*, whether they be Human or alien. It is the one trait all intelligent life forms have in common. This spiritual gift establishes the very foundation on how to search for intelligent alien life.

Spiritual Categories Of Imago-Dei Alien Life

If God chose to create alien intelligent life, they too must possess both material and immaterial properties. This

---

[169] Ibid. (p.157)

does not mean they would look human, but like humans, they would have a body and a soul with the gift of *imago Dei*. They would possess dual natures. The immaterial aspect of their dual nature reflects the image of God and this essence is given by God. This is crucial. So, intelligent life, no matter the planet, is actually *imago Dei* life.

Having *imago Dei* in common among all intelligent life forms is critical in searching for alien intelligent life. This commonality establishes key universal categories about intelligent life, which will prove critical in knowing where to search for them. As we have seen in our own history, *imago Dei* beings fall into one of five spiritual categories:

1. Beings that have not Fallen. *i.e. pure, innocent*

2. Beings that are in the process of Falling. *i.e. rebellious, stupid*

3. Beings that have Fallen. *i.e. depraved, lost, perverted, corrupt*

4. Beings that are in the process of being restored to God. *i.e. redeemed, saved*

5. Beings that are fully restored to God. *i.e. glorified, refined*

For humans, category one covers six days (Genesis 1 and 2); category two covers six verses (Genesis 3:1–6); and category three covers six words, *"...she took some and ate it."* (Genesis 3:6a). Category four begins the dramatic saga of God redeeming His lost race of humans, which begins in earnest in Genesis chapter twelve. It is here where Abraham is kept from slaying his only son; it is here that

God introduces the forgiveness of sins through human sacrifice for the first time. This theme and theology climaxes at the Roman cross where Jesus Christ suffered, died and was buried only to rise up out of the grave and ascend into heaven for you and me. This redemption story penned in Scripture covers sixteen hundred years of human history, involving cultures from five continents in three languages. All this to usher humanity to category five and that which all Christians yearn for—our Hope: *"Then I saw a new Heaven and New Earth..."* John's revelation, written from a vision he had while exiled on the island of Patmos, closes out an epic romance between God and the children of God. A tale of kings and queens, treason and murder, cowardice and hatred, heroes and villains, forgiveness and love, and battles won against all odds. After all this, notice where the final chapter in this great saga ends, just like it begins, pointing us up to the Heavens. In the case of intelligent alien life, no matter the category they might be in, they too have an epic God story.

It is these universal spiritual categories that hold the key on where to search for intelligent alien life.

The Treacherous Key Variable

If we take the Genesis account of Creation seriously—meaning a literal rebellion from God—it reveals that *imago Dei* life is vulnerable to sin. Although sin is a metaphysical (moral) property of life; it still has a devastating impact on NASA's quest to find intelligent alien life on other Earths. Sin is the treacherous key. This treachery may begin in the metaphysical but ultimately manifests itself in the physical. The most recognized physical manifestation of sin known in science today is the Second Law of Thermodynamics: Entropy.

Entropy is a Greek word meaning "transformation," coined by Rudolf Clausius (1822–1888).[170] It explains how everything is decaying. All orderly systems are breaking down into chaos. All things, when left to themselves, will fail. This process is evident throughout nature from the smallest atom to my now lukewarm cup of coffee, to stars burning out and even the universe breaking down and fading into a cold oblivion.[171] American historian, Henry Adams (1838–1918), had this to say about entropy, *...for the layman this only means that the heap of ashes becomes ever bigger.*

Australian physicist, Johannes Joseph Loschmidt, upon reading Clausius' equations on entropy, deplored: *The terroristic nimbus of the second law...a destructive principle of all life in the universe.*[172] We see such evidence of physical decay all around us.[173] It is the Fall that introduced the Second Law of Thermodynamics. We see in Genesis how entropy did not exist in the Garden of Eden. There was no death. Yet, we know entropy to exist all around us. We no longer exist in the flawless Garden of Eden, but in the broken wilderness as Scripture reveals:

> *So the LORD God banished him from the Garden of Eden to work the ground from which he had been taken. After he drove the man out, he placed on the east*

---

[170] Ben-Naim, Arieh. *Entropy Demystified*. World Scientific: Hackensack, 2008. Print.

[171] Goldstein, M., I. Goldstein. *The Refrigerator and the Universe, Understanding the Laws of Energy*. Harvard University Press: London, 2003. Print. (p.387-388)

[172] Muller, Ingo, Weiss, Wolf. *Entropy and Energy: A Universal Competition*. Springer-Verlaag: Berlin, 2005. Print. (p.233)

[173] Some modern biblical scholars argue against the physical effects of the Fall in order for their end-time theology to work. This will be touched on in chapter twelve.

> *side of the Garden of Eden cherubim and a flaming sword flashing back and forth to guard the way... (Gen 3:23–24)*

An astrophysicist would call this "wilderness" a parallel reality, another dimension, or a multiverse as String Theory postulates. Humans have been torn away from God's Creation that He called *good*[174] and into a corrupted copy where sin/entropy (sintropy) runs rampant.

And this is why the *imago Dei* nature of intelligent life plays such a key role in any attempts to make first contact with intelligent aliens:

First, if God created intelligent aliens and they have not fallen, then they remain in God's *good* Creation...where we are no longer.

Second, if God created intelligent aliens and they fell into sin, then they have been torn away from God's *good* Creation into their own corrupt parallel reality unique to their sin. They are separated from God and from us.

Think of a parallel reality as Stephen Hawking did; he referred to each layer of reality as a "brane."[175] Or think of it as the prophet Isaiah did; he thought of our reality as a thin scroll momentarily unfurled:

> *All the stars in the sky will be dissolved and the heavens rolled up like a scroll... (Isaiah 34:4)*

---

[174] Genesis 1:31–2:1: "God saw all that he had made, and it was **very good**. And there was evening, and there was morning—the sixth day. Thus the heavens and the earth were completed in all their vast array." [bold mine]

[175] Hawking, Stephen. *Universe in a Nutshell.* A Bantam Book: New York, 2001. Print.

This idea has been around for thousands of years as seen in Scripture, but it is not how the 21st century mind typically thinks of reality. To help further explain this idea of a corrupted parallel universe, consider this short narrative about sin-fallen aliens discovering our Earth…

For centuries they walked with God until the Fall. For eons since, they yearned as the stars taunted them, feeling lost and longing to understand their place in it all. As their super-giant star basked them in brilliant blue-white light, so it also marked the seasons and the ages that past. Eventually, they advanced beyond their skies and observed an average yellow-star far away that dips in brightness at regular intervals. Upon closer scrutiny they found this star hosts a solar system of eight planets and one of them, the third one, is within the stars habitable zone. At great cost to their species, they erected a larger more powerful space-telescope to scour this new found habitable world for signatures of life…and found it. This epic moment boosts a century long obsession forgetting their sick, their dying, their starving; in order to develop new technology to take them there. This new technology actually unifies the trinity of forces, folding space-time into a singularity, cheating space of its vast distance and making time inconsequential. At long last, this new world is just a step away. Under great fanfare the heroic crew walk through, stepping onto this small alien planet eerily bathed in the warmth of a yellow star. As their Jupiter-like world watches, the captain confirms the atmosphere to be breathable and draws a deep breath of pristine air. A short recon reveals wild, uncared for alien vegetation and a world teeming with strange creatures. The captain then mobilizes highly organized teams to seek out intelligent life. Days turn into months, turn into years and their hopes fade. Finally, with great despair, she announces to their world in waiting that they are alone—that there has never been intelligent life on Earth.

This is what I mean by a parallel universe. Everything is the same in each universe except *imago Dei* life. Because of this mysterious *imago Dei* component of intelligent life, intelligent life is vulnerable to one thing that lower life forms and higher life forms do not have to contend with: sin. Sin is a spiritual condition that causes a physical condition known as Entropy. Sin separates *imago Dei* life from God. Entropy separates *imago Dei* life from God's *good* Creation. God's *good* Creation is where non-fallen and fully redeemed *imago Dei* life exists. NASA's telescopes and spacecrafts are not equipped to see God's "good" creation. And God would not allow sinful humans and there technology to pierce His *good* creation. It would be like matter and anti-matter colliding in the LHC; a violent annihilation would be the result.

God's *good* Creation is first seen in the Bible's book of Genesis in the very first chapters:

> *God saw all that he had made, and it was very good. (Genesis 1:31a)*

And sin removed humans from His *good* creation as revealed in Genesis chapter three,

> *So the LORD God banished him from the Garden of Eden to work the ground from which he had been taken. ^{24} After he drove the man out, he placed on the east side[e] of the Garden of Eden cherubim and a flaming sword flashing back and forth to guard the way to the tree of life. (Genesis 3:23-24)*

To keep this verse in context, it is referring to Adam and Eve walking out of the Garden of Eden into the dessert.[176] However, this literal act of banishment symbolizes the act of leaving God's *good* creation and stepping into a corrupted parallel reality. The moment they stepped out of the Garden, they stepped into a corrupted parallel world. A window between worlds, which quantum physics and String Theory supports. The author of Genesis further reveals blazing swords splitting these two realms apart. Sin ushered our ancestors into a corrupted parallel universe where Entropy rules. This parallel realm looks the same as God's *good* creation, including the plants and animals, but like my short-story reveals, plants and animals are all that there is. *Imago Dei* life that caused the sin will be the only *imago Dei* life in that sinverse. God is a Just God. *Imago Dei* life that has not fallen will not be condemned by God to exist in a fallen realm. And finally, it would be unjust of God to sentence humans to exist in a fallen sinverse that humans did not cause. The aliens in my short story sinned and their sin is not "our" sin.

So NASA's Discovery Class of Missions, which includes Kepler and the James Webb, will not find other intelligent life in our sinverse. NASA would need to develop technology that can actually breach each fallen parallel universe to search for intelligent alien life. But

---

[176] If the garden were to exist today, which it doesn't, it would be in modern day Iraq.

there is a holy reason why "we" are separated from God and all other fallen *imago Dei* life. I can't help but think of the Tower of Babel account in scripture. It was also created to breach the heavens.

> *⁴ Then they said, "Come, let us build ourselves a city, with a tower that reaches to the heavens, so that we may make a name for ourselves; otherwise we will be scattered over the face of the whole earth."⁵ But the LORD came down to see the city and the tower the people were building. ⁶ The LORD said, "If as one people speaking the same language they have begun to do this, then nothing they plan to do will be impossible for them. ⁷ Come, let us go down and confuse their language so they will not understand each other."⁸ So the LORD scattered them from there over all the earth, and they stopped building the city. (Genesis 11:3-9)*

God frustrated that ancient project to keep it from continuing. I believe it would be the same with any human attempt to develop the technology for first contact with an alien race. They have been separated for a purpose, as have we.

So, NASA's 2018 launch of the gold-plated James Webb Space Telescope may identify signatures of life in Kepler's new found habitable worlds, but those signatures will only be from lower life forms like plants and animals. And when I say "signatures," I mean by-products created from living things such as methane, carbon-dioxide and oxygen. No signatures will emanate from intelligent life forms. Our fallen nature separates us from them. Sin phased us into our own corrupted universe in the blink of an eye. Therefore, I say this with great sorrow in my heart, but unfortunately, NASA and SETI's diligent quests to make first contact with intelligent alien life is in vain. They are searching in the wrong realm.

However, I should note that my theology on alien *imago Dei* life is not that of Dorothy Chappell and E. David Cook's. In their book they carefully craft this statement on the subject of alien life:

> *There is reason to believe that with such an enormous universe and countless planets around other stars, God may be interacting with life forms we can only dream about.*[177]

If by "interacting" they mean God is talking to, relating with and walking by the side of; and if by "life forms" they mean intelligent alien life; then they fail to take *imago Dei* and the Fall seriously. In a nutshell, alien *imago Dei* will either be fallen or not fallen. If they are not fallen, they are with God in His *good* Creation where we are no longer. If they are fallen, then they are skewed slightly out of phase and reside in their own sinverse. In either case, they are not in our reality as Chappell and Cook seem to indicate. They also fail to seriously consider the catastrophic physical ramifications of the Fall. As revealed throughout the Bible, the Fall affected everything. And I do mean everything. Consider Job 25:5, where it declares, *...the stars are not pure in God's eyes...* and in the New Testament the Apostle Paul states, *...the creation was subjected to frustration, not by its own choice,* and later states Creation to be in *...bondage to decay...*(Romans

---

[177] Chappell, Dorothy, David E. Cook. *Not Just Science.* Zondervan: Grand Rapids, 2005. Print. (p.105)

8:20–22), which we observe as entropy. Depravity has physically altered our space-time dimension. Our entire universe has been subjected to frustration, decay, and eventual utter death. God created a *good* universe and placed humans in it as seen in Genesis one and two. But humans sinned, causing God to exile sinful humans from a sinless place. We now exist in an alternate universe that cosmologists and String Theory would refer to as a parallel universe or multiverse.

And this is what grips my soul every time I ponder the stars through my telescope: These ancient carriers of light only exist now to remind us of what we could have had. They only serve to tease us. Our heavenly Father created a never-ending universe for an everlasting people. His good Creation was ours to discover and enjoy. But, we threw it all away…for this.

God has been creating since eternity-past and will keep on creating for all eternity-future. If somewhere in all of eternity-past God created alien *imago Dei* beings who also sinned, it begs the next question: *Would they know Jesus?*

8. WOULD THEY KNOW JESUS

Their hearts leaped and a wild hope rose within them. ...The dream is ended: this is the morning.' And as He spoke He no longer looked to them like a lion...

~C.S. Lewis
(1898–1963)
*The Chronicles of Narnia,
The Last Journey*

Who am I when I consider this tiny blue dot orbiting a star one hundred times its size.[178] Who am I, when the next closest star, Proxima Centauri, is 24 trillion miles away, taking over 10,000 years to reach with our fastest spaceship design.[179] Who am I, when our Sun is one of 400 billion Suns in our galaxy. Who am I, when our galaxy is lost among a dozen galaxies within our Local Cluster that is gravitationally locked to a thousand more galaxies in the Virgo Super Cluster. Who am I, when our super cluster is rocketing through deep space at 13 million mph toward an unseen destination known as The Great Attractor.[180] Who am I? Insignificant. I am insignificant on an absurdly vast scale. At least, that is the answer from modern science.

---

[178] Rounded out for the sake of clarity.
[179] Hawking, Stephen. A *Briefer History of Time*. Bantam Books: New York, 2005. Print. (p.4)
[180] From our perspective the Local and Super Cluster of galaxies are being drawn toward an unseen location 7 degrees above our galactic plane. If you look just above-right of the constellation Sagittarius, our galaxy and thousands of others are being drawn in this general direction toward something astronomers call, *"The Great Attractor."*

But, if we expand upon an earlier thought by Sagan, it would indeed be "...conceited of us..." to think that God Almighty did nothing on the eighth day nor before the first day. Surely, boredom was not the catalyst for thrusting forth Creation. Since Creator God has probably been creating for all eternity past and for all eternity future, then how does Jesus Christ play into these other possible creations? Our Bible teaches us that there is only one Jesus, who was born on Earth, and who only had to die once for all humans (1 Peter 3:18). If any other intelligent beings exist in other realms in eternity past or eternity future, must they then know the Son of Man from Nazareth?

We would not have the theological base to discuss the possible existence of alien *imago Dei* beings without standing on the shoulders of great theologians who discovered that Jesus Christ has a dual nature and that God is a Triune God. Systematic theology was once the king of the sciences, founded by brilliant men like Origen of Alexandria (185–254 A.D.), the father of systematic theology who resided in the famous School Of Alexandria, Egypt. This school was once the world-renown center of western thought and philosophy for more than three hundred years. The School Of Alexandria drew a wealth of knowledge from one of the seven wonders of the ancient world: the Royal Library of Alexandria. This extensive library contained ancient texts from the dawn of writing that scholars today can only dream of and still lament over their loss to fire. Many historians debate how it came to ruin, but one thing is certain—when it fell, Rome eventually fell too, setting back western culture and technology over a thousand years. Such a center of learning and academia can never be replaced, but the one saving grace were the Christian monks salvaging some of ancient academia and hiding away in their enclaves across Europe to continue the work founded by Origen, Augustine,

Irenaeus, and so many other early church fathers. These enclaves went on to produce the most profound truths in Christian thought that helped develop western thought and culture we know today. It is here, or I should say then, that we must look in order to continue our discussion of alien *imago Dei* life and if they would know Jesus.

Son of Man / Son of God

The title, "Son of Man" was Jesus' favorite reference when referring to Himself, and used eighty-six times in the New Testament,

> *The Son of Man must be delivered into the hands of sinful men, be crucified and on the third day be raised again. (Luke 24:7).*

The era that Jesus and the apostles lived was a time of Greek gods, who loomed ever present in the minds of the Greco-Roman citizens. The apostle Paul recorded in Scripture how the people even once declared him and his fellow healer to be gods cloaked in human-like form and wanted to erect statues of them for worship:

> *When the crowd saw what Paul had done, they shouted in the Lycaonian language, "The gods have come down to us in human form!" Barnabas they called Zeus, and Paul they called Hermes because he was the chief speaker. (Acts 4:11)*

Such pagan ideas had to be overcome, and the key to overcoming them is dualism—that Jesus Christ is fully God and fully human. He is therefore not a demi-god or one of many gods but *thee* God. This duality allows Jesus, being fully human, to be the appropriate sacrifice for all humans, and being fully God, to have the power and might to overcome death. If He isn't fully human, Jesus would not be the acceptable ransom in our place. Human beings would have no hope of being freed from our sin and misery. And, if Jesus isn't fully God, then the remarkable proclamations He makes about Himself would make him a lunatic. The distinction in His duality is critical in the discussion of aliens and Jesus.

Since Jesus, the Son of Man, is the perfect blood sacrifice for humans, this then means that He cannot be the perfect blood sacrifice for non-humans. Alien intelligent life are not human, not our flesh and blood. They would need God to provide a savior in their flesh and blood. This is where the Trinity shines glorious and eternal, transcending our space-time. The Son of Man is also the second person of the Trinity: the Son of God. The Son of God is eternally begotten not made. This is Christian doctrine as found in the famous Apostles Creed. So, the son of God was never born but always was and is and is come. The Son of God is eternal.[181] The Bible allows us a glimpse of this when Jesus proclaims to His disciples, *"You are from below, I am from above; you are from this world, I am not from this world" (John 8:23)*. What Jesus is distinguishing in this shocking statement is His duality: Son of God/Son of Man. In this case, He was referring to His divine nature as Son of God, pre-existing and transcending our space-time dimension. One notices how careful Jesus is with whom He entrusts this revelation. Another glimpse into this duality occurs after He sent out 72 of his finest to surrounding towns proclaiming the good news and healing the sick in His name. When His disciples returned, they were quite excited, and in this party-ish atmosphere, Jesus revealed something amazing about Himself:

---

[181] Revelation 1:8

> *All things have been committed to me by my Father. No one knows who the Son is except the Father, and no one knows who the Father is except the Son and those to whom the Son chooses to reveal him. Then he turned to his disciples and said privately, "Blessed are the eyes that see what you see. For I tell you that many prophets and kings wanted to see what you see but did not see it, and to hear what you hear but did not hear it. (Luke 10:22–24)*

What they see is the Son of Man, but what they experience is the Son of God.

The Son of God is there at Genesis one creating *(John 1:3a)*, while the Son of Man was born on Earth *(John 1:14a)*. Since humans are created from the dust of Earth, that makes Jesus an Earthling. So the question, "Would they know Jesus?" is theologically flawed. The motive behind the question is good, but the question reveals a poor understanding of Christ's duality and a somewhat conceited "center-of-the-universe" mentality. The question implies that all of God's creatures throughout all of eternity past and future must know a human from Earth for salvation. How small and narrow we view our Creator God and how lofty we consider ourselves. We must humble ourselves, and science tends to help us in this area, to admit that we are not all that there is. God existed for all eternity and therefore transcends our existence and even our space-time. The duality of Christ and the reality of the Trinity provides hope for all *imago Dei* life no matter where and when they are. The Son of God is there to redeem those that have rebelled, becoming their perfect savior in their flesh in their sinverse wilderness.

Nestorius

Some bible scholars may think of Nestorius, the Bishop of Constantinople, when reading these distinctions on Christ's duality. Nestorianism was intensely debated during the Council of Ephesus in 431 A.D., finally concluding that this distinction is dangerous, for it emphasizes the two persons of Jesus more than it emphasizes Jesus as one. I agree with the Church Fathers that Nestorianism is a heresy when discussing it within the context of our space-time universe, but this is not the context here. I am talking about non-human *imago Dei* life outside of our space-time. They would not fall under our esteemed Church Fathers' definition of heresy. Perhaps, Nestorius was a faithful bishop way ahead of his time; when light from a hundred thousand stars were still fifteen hundred years from revealing the need of such an understanding. As NASA pushes the envelope of human understanding with so many brave new worlds already discovered, it is our responsibility as Christians to be prepared. The Bible puts it this way: *"But in your hearts set apart Christ as Lord. Always be prepared to give an answer to everyone who asks you to give the reason for the hope that you have" (1 Peter 3:15).* It seems our Christian worldview is in need of a Christian Spaceview.

PART III

A CHRISTIAN SPACEVIEW

God is not like a human being; it is not important for God to have visible evidence so that he can see if his cause has been victorious or not; he sees in secret just as well.

~ Søren Kierkegaard
(1813–1855)

9. FAITH: A CHRISTIAN SPACEVIEW

Science without religion is lame. But religion without science is blind.

~Albert Einstein
(1879–1955)

For the first time in human history, science has provided the means to answer two profound questions: *Are there other habitable worlds like Earth? Does alien life exist?* NASA's Kepler Science Team is now answering the first question. The second age-old question teeters upon the completion and launch of NASA's James Webb Space Telescope. Pushed back to a 2018 launch date, this gold-plated infrared telescope is capable of analyzing the atmospheres of Kepler's new worlds for signatures of life. Such discoveries are equivalent to Christopher Columbus discovering the "new world." These epic moments in history stoke the fires of god-less interpretations on what such findings mean via every major media outlet across the globe. And their message appears to be the same: habitable worlds are natural, they do not need a Creator. The time has come for our Christian Worldview to gain a Christian Spaceview.

Five Truths

There are five truths in a Christian Spaceview to combat this god-less rhetoric. These truths support one guiding principle for a Christian's life in this space age we now live in: *Science has nothing to do with **what** we believe in, but in better understanding **Who** we believe in.*

First Truth

The first Christian Spaceview truth: conflict is okay; it should be embraced and not avoided. Many people find themselves embroiled in a silent conflict between science and faith. Do not frame it as an ultimatum. If you think about conflict, Newton's classical physics conflicts with Einstein's relativity physics, which conflicts with quantum physics. One branch of science conflicts with other branches of science. For that matter, Republicans conflict with Democrats, Catholics with Protestants...all the way down to cats with dogs. The fact that you might have conflict in your life simply confirms that you are alive. Conflict is in everything and in everyone in our sinverse. In the case of the highly anticipated discoveries coming from the Kepler Mission, the conflict should not be an internal one about what you believe: science or faith. Instead, the conflict should be an external one about how scientists are *interpreting* the discoveries of habitable worlds. Their interpretations reveal their god-less personal bias. Their interpretations are subjective, not objective.

Second Truth

Second truth for a Christian Spaceview: the strength of your faith is not built on piety. Piety is well illustrated in the Bible by the religious leaders of Jesus day, the ones he yelled at:

> *Woe to you, teachers of the law and Pharisees, you hypocrites! You are like whitewashed tombs, which look beautiful on the outside but on the inside are full of dead men's bones and everything unclean. In the same way, on the outside you appear to people as righteous but on the inside you are*

> *full of hypocrisy and wickedness. (Matthew 23:27–28)*

Piety today is seen in those who take pride in how they look, speak, and act. For Christians this would be about wearing the proper outfits, an immaculate car, and proper lingo on Sunday morning. All such trappings imply that faith isn't enough but that one must also act a certain narrowly defined way. The great 20th century theologian, Karl Barth, stated: *"Piety has nothing to do with faith."* Just be yourself. Live life! Don't live to show how good you can act, such piety Jesus labeled hypocritical.

Third Truth

Third truth for a Christian Spaceview is broken-down into two sections: Context and Reasoned Faith. An unshakeable Christian faith is built on these.

> *Now the Bereans were of more noble character than the Thessalonians, for they received the message with great eagerness and examined the Scriptures every day to see if what Paul said was true. (Acts 17:11–12)*

Studying God's word correctly develops a deep understanding and unshakeable faith. But be careful here, just because one reads their Bible every day does not mean they are interpreting it correctly, and it may just mean they are pious. Misinterpreting Scripture is common and leaves one vulnerable to piety, arrogance, or superstition. In contrast, properly understanding God's Holy Word gives the reader confidence and peace. These five steps will get you on the road to understanding God's Word in its proper context:

Context

1. Grammar: The Bible was written in two chief languages, Hebrew (Old Testament) and Greek (New Testament). These human languages follow human rules that must be followed for a proper understanding of what is being communicated, known as syntax. You do not need to learn Greek and Hebrew. With your Bible in hand, first identify the subject of the sentence, the verb, the direct object and any prepositional phrases. This is vital. Then define these key words as they were defined in the time the word was chosen by the translators and not by what the word means today. This is known as etymology. A famous example of how a word's meaning changes over time is well illustrated when reporters asked Sir Arthur C. Clarke, the famous sci-fi writer, if he is gay. He would respond, *"no, merely cheerful."*[182] The word "gay" changed from meaning cheerful when Clarke was a boy to meaning homosexual. It is worth noting here that you do not need to learn the original languages, though it is a rich blessing to do so. A good Bible dictionary is a great tool as well.

2. Genre (jon-rah): This identifies the style of writing. The Bible employs five basic styles of writing: narrative, poetry, letter, apocalyptic, historical. In general, assume the words and events are literal (real events

---

[182] Luke Harding, The Guardian Article History, 9/28/00, www.guardian.co.uk. Web.

that actually occurred in history) unless the writer indicates otherwise. The only exception to this rule is apocalyptic literature and poetry. For example, if the biblical author designates that he is writing a psalm, treat it as song/poetry and learn the forms of song and poetry used back in that era. Do not use poetry and song as literal historical accounts. A good example of this is the famous song written and sung by Gordon Lightfoot about the sinking of the Edmund Fitzgerald in Lake Superior. I took my family around Shipwreck Point on our boat and there at the point is the Shipwreck Museum and lighthouse. It is in this museum where recovered items from the Edmund Fitzgerald now rest and where this song is played over and over again. The song is a dramatic retelling of the event that evokes feelings to help us remember the ship and its crew, but after visiting the museum and learning about the event, one realizes just how un-factual the song is. The power of song and poetry causes events to become larger than life and therefore remembered, whereas a factual accounting is easily forgotten due to a lack of inspiration. This is also true of poetry and song in Scripture. It isn't errant, because the feelings and inspiration it evokes are true, which is its purpose. If it was meant to be literal and factual, it wouldn't be a song or poem.

3. Historicity: The inspired human writers did not write in a vacuum, but wrote within the setting of their culture. We must resist

interpreting Scripture from our cultural point of view. The best way to avoid this is to understand each writer's culture, which is made up of geography, politics, religions of the day, customs and there economy. The best way to do this is to read books by archeologists, but the fun and more impacting way is to go there! The text will become easier to understand and more meaningful by hiking the hills, seeing the lay of the land, walking the actual roadways, and meeting the people.

4. Context: look at the verses before it and the verses after it to get the bigger picture. Consider the historicity, genre, and grammar as discussed earlier. Take in the whole picture then read the verse. For example: *"At the end of every seven years you must cancel debts."* By knowing this verse came from Deuteronomy and that it is in the Old Testament, helps identify who the writer was writing to—Hebrews. Not Americans. This is context.

5. Exposition: Once the above steps have been done, then rephrase the message into the appropriate modern day way of talking/writing to help fully appreciate the truth. If all the other steps are followed, but fail to translate what you have learned into today's words, the full meaning will not be fully appreciated.

Being equipped with these powerful tools helps keep each verse in God's Word in proper context, to be applied as it was intended, instead of however we want it to. Having established a proper understanding of the Word of God assures a firm faith in Genesis and the rest of the Bible—no matter what the mainstream media tries to trip you up with.

Reasoned Faith

Continuing on the third truth, here are some key scriptures and quotes from famous saints to help recognize how faith and reason work together:

> Isaiah the Prophet:
> *'Come now, let us reason together,' says the LORD. (Isaiah 1:18)*
>
> King David:
> *He who gets wisdom loves his own soul; he who cherishes understanding prospers. (Proverbs 19:8)*
>
> Paul the Apostle:
> *As his custom was, Paul went into the synagogue, and on three Sabbath days he reasoned with them from the scriptures. (Acts 17:2)*
>
> John Calvin:
> *[Faith is] a firm and certain knowledge of God's benevolence towards us.*[183]
>
> C.S. Lewis:

---

[183] Plantinga, Alvin. *Religion and Science*. 20 Feb. 2007. Web. <http://www.plato.cstanford.edu>

> *...the virtue by which we hold to our reasoned ideas, despite mood to the contrary.*

And finally, consider this account of a military leader in the Gospels. Does this respected leader exercise blind faith or reasoned faith:

> *The centurion replied, "Lord, I do not deserve to have you come under my roof. But just say the word, and my servant will be healed. For I myself am a man under authority, with soldiers under me. I tell this one, 'Go,' and he goes; and that one, 'Come,' and he comes. I say to my servant, 'Do this,' and he does it." When Jesus heard this, he was astonished and said to those following him, "I tell you the truth, I have not found anyone in Israel with such great faith...Then Jesus said to the Centurion, "Go! It will be done just as you believed it would." And his servant was healed at that very hour. (Matthew 8:8–13)*

First, the Centurion knew *who* Jesus was, nobody had to introduce him, which indicates he must have observed Jesus before this encounter. Second and finally, the Centurion knew the general location of *where* Jesus was, meaning that he had been keeping track of Him, maybe out of duty or perhaps out of interest. If we put these clues together, the Roman Centurion had already made up his mind before this event took place based on what he had heard, at minimum, and most likely had seen. He believed in Jesus from the information he had gathered. This famous account of Jesus and the soldier reveals that faith requires the gathering of information and then choosing to act upon it. One cannot make a decision if they have no information to even know a decision must be made. Faith requires the gathering of information first and then making a reasoned judgment. Just like science requires reason, so does faith.

Fourth Truth

The fourth truth in a Christian Spaceview: Blind faith does not exist. A person must first become aware in something or in someone before they can choose to believe or not believe. So faith, in anything, first requires information. We will first discuss this idea as it applies to Christian faith and then as it applies to scientific endeavor.

Unfortunately, many Christians say they believe in blind faith. Some of the most common verses used in the New Testament on this nonsensical and shallow idea of faith are:

We live by faith, not by sight. (2 Corinthians 5:7)

...faith is being sure of what we hope for and certain of what we do not see. (Hebrews 11:1)

...blessed are those who have not seen and yet have believed. (John 20:29)

To properly understand these verses we must understand the context in which they were written. To illustrate, let's talk "PB&J." There is nothing better than spreading warm smooth peanut butter and cold grape jelly on two slices of soft white bread. Add a fresh bag of salty potato chips and chocolate milk and you have "manna from heaven." But peanut butter and jelly without the bread sandwiching it would be a mess, and that is how these verses have been treated when people reference them as proof of "blind faith." These verses, as all of Scripture, must be sandwiched. In the case of, *"We live by faith, not by sight,"* the verses before and after are looking ahead to the hope of being in heaven with a new body, one that does not ache and cause us to groan from growing old. This short verse is not about blind faith but having faith that this aging body and skewed reality is only temporary. It is having faith in something.

In the second misunderstood verse, *"...faith is being sure of what we hope for and certain of what we do not see,"* Paul spends the rest of that chapter recalling famous Bible characters, ranging from Moses to a prostitute, and their demonstrations of faith. No blind faith here since demonstrations of faith are anything but. Our faith is based on thousands of years of world famous people who believe in God and demonstrated their faith and became famous in doing so and are now household names. Faith in Christ is never blind, thanks to this *great cloud of witnesses* that we can read about.

In the final misunderstood verse, *"blessed are those who have not seen and yet have believed,"* many people make the mistake of using this verse as a verse just for you and me today. Look at that verse and ask yourself, Is it set in the past tense, present tense, or future tense? The verbiage is past tense. Jesus is referring to those who have already trusted in Him. This verse is as far as you can get on the idea of "blind faith" since Jesus is referring to people that are there with Him in His day and age that have seen Him, touched Him and watched Him perform countless miracles first hand!

And these three verses are the ones that seem to get the greatest attention, never mind the couple hundred other verses on faith in the New Testament to the contrary. The Apostle Paul sums it up well:

> *...and how can they believe in him if they have never heard about him? And how can they hear about him unless someone tells them? (Romans 10:14b NLT)*

Do this simple experiment; ask anyone what faith is. Go ahead, try it! You'll get answers with the word or idea of "blind" in it. But, those with a proper understanding of Scripture, and therefore of faith, will prove unmovable in what they believe. They will find scientific discovery to be a ticket to adventure, keeping an open mind, unafraid of what is discovered next as it only serves to be a catalyst for digging deeper into understanding God's great Creation.

Now about faith as it applies to scientific endeavor. A Christian Spaceview also recognizes that even god-less scientists still employ fundamental belief systems, *i.e. faith.* Michael Polanyi (1891–1976), a brilliant and decorated scientist coined the term *Tacit Knowledge* to explain how even science is rooted in belief systems. In a nutshell, he explains that a scientist gathers information and then establishes what they *believe* it means for discovering something new...something yet unknown that they believe is out there. *E.g. Dark Matter, Dark Energy or the Higgs boson particle.* And then based on this belief, they choose to methodically pursue it.

So, let me quickly recap before I present the fifth and final Christian Spaceview truth. First, conflict is okay; it should not be avoided but embraced. Second, piety is not equal to faith. Third, Context & Reasoned Faith. Fourth, blind faith does not exist. Now for the final truth.

Fifth Truth

The fifth and final truth for a Christian Spaceview is to recognize the difference between the scientific discovery and how scientists *interpret* the scientific discovery. Recognizing the difference between the discovery and the interpretation of the discovery is absolutely critical. Kepler's discovery of other habitable worlds like Earth is only a matter of time and this should not be where the conflict is as a Christian. Instead, the conflict should be in the *interpretation* presented by god-less scientists and the mainstream media. The mainstream media has been and will continue to present only those scientists with god-less worldviews—void of direction and purpose and rich in fatalistic notions cloaked as science. If one fails to recognize that these scientists are presenting subjective interpretations[184] of the discovery, then that person is being duped. Do not be duped.

Those who do not realize these five truths will find a deep conflict stirring within them. Those who apply these truths will enjoy a firm faith against such god-less rhetoric cloaked as science. Not only is their faith unmoved, but they will find themselves able to delve into the excitement of the latest scientific discoveries instead of shying away from them—leading themselves, and others, to celebrate the wonder of God's creation. Legitimate science can actually serve as a catalyst that draws one to deeper faith. Theologians call this the Teleological Argument. I call it accountability. We no longer believe the Earth is the center of the universe—thanks to science. Galileo famously weighed in on this saying to Cardinal Baronius of the

---

[184] Even modern science practices subjectivity. Proof of this is Einstein's famous "blunder", the "cosmological constant," a constant he added in his General Theory of Relativity due to his belief the universe is unchanging.

Inquisition, "The Bible teaches us how to go to heaven, not how the heavens go."[185] Cardinal Baronius, however, was not amused.

Famous author, C.S. Lewis, made the attempt to bridge the understanding between faith and science in his sci-fi trilogy: *Out of the Silent Planet, Perelandra*, and *That Hideous Strength* in the 1930s. In these books, a human transports to Mars and another to Venus (respectively) only to find different outcomes of their "Adams" and "Eves." The first book has Earthlings actually discovering alien life on Mars and as the story progresses, the Martians named our world "the silent planet" because humans will not testify that Jesus Christ is the creator of all things. In *Perelandra*, the author does the unexpected and has the character from Earth, who is fallen, go to the rescue of the "Adam" and "Eve" on Venus, who are on the verge of falling. With much drama, the Earthling succeeds in his righteous plot to kill the tempter, thereby saving the Venetians' first parents. I find the end fascinating and still pondering it, but more important is what C.S. Lewis was trying to do. He attempted to open the discussion with Christians about the idea of other habitable worlds and alien life while integrating science into the faith discussion. But it never took. I mean, have you heard of these books? Even so, science helps faith. Take astronomy for example, the study of the cosmos. I have found that the more I study this ancient testament of God's, the greater I marvel over our omnipotent Creator. It encourages and inspires my faith. Thomas Aquinas championed this notion of the natural order declaring God's presence, and made it his life's work to develop a systematic theology the Roman Catholic Church adheres to known as Natural Theology.[186]

---

[185] Kaku, Michio. *Parallel Worlds*. DoubleDay: New York, 2005. Print. (p.343)
[186] Protestant theologians are unanimous that Natural Theology is

So let your mind imagine amazing things, like a planet so huge that it could hold dozens of Earths, yet so light it could float on water. You just imagined Saturn. You see, there's a good chance in an infinite universe created by an all-knowing God, that anything is possible. And like faith bending our minds to believe in walking through doors and walking on water; science too pushes us beyond our wildest imaginations like the very real possibility of many other Earths and alien life. The Vatican hosted a five day conference in November, 2009, at Vatican City on the subject of other planets and alien life in light of NASA's mission. Their Chief Astronomer, Rev. Jose Gabriel Funes, stated at the conference,

> *Just as there is a multitude of creatures on Earth, there could be other beings, even intelligent ones, created by God. This does not contradict our faith, because we cannot put limits on God's creative freedom.* [187]

So a Christian Spaceview of faith recognizes these five truths and one guiding principle:

- Conflict is okay; it should be embraced and not avoided. It is a part of life.
- There is no room for piety. Jesus disdained "whitewashed tombs"[188] and enjoyed hanging out with

---

fatally flawed as it pertains to a person's salvation (Special Revelation), but generally agree with Aquinas as it pertains to General Revelation.

[187] Krauss, Russell. "Vatican Hosts Conference on Alien Life." Boise Liberal Examiner 15 Nov. 2009, Web. 15 Nov. 2009.
<http://www.examiner.com/x-6186-Boise-Liberal-Examiner~y2009m11d15-Vatican-hosts-conference-on-alien-worlds-alien-life.html>

[188] Matt 23:27: "Woe to you, teachers of the law and Pharisees, you hypocrites! You are like whitewashed tombs, which look beautiful on

people who were just being themselves, instead of acting.
- Reasoned faith is built out of studying God's Word, properly, understanding the context. This assures peace of mind and surety of faith instead of arrogance or superstition.
- There is no such thing as blind faith. Blind faith does not exist.
- There is an important difference between the discovery and the interpretation of the discovery.

And finally, a Christian Spaceview exercises this guiding principle: *Science has nothing to do with **what** we believe in, but in better understanding **Who** we believe in.*

---

the outside but on the inside are full of dead men's bones and everything unclean."

10. TIME: A CHRISTIAN SPACEVIEW

The universe has a design, and so does a book. But unlike the universe, a book does not appear spontaneously from nothing. A book requires a creator.

*~Stephen Hawking
Mathematician/Cosmologist/Author/Atheist*

The sheer size of it in the middle of the desert was other worldly. I kept gawking at it, stunned at the mountain of concrete filling the valley before me. On a business trip to Vegas, I was able to finish early and scoot out to the Hoover Dam. I knew it was big, but to this day, even as I write this, I still feel the grand sense it evoked when I stood there trying to take it all in—truly one of the modern wonders. Think of an experience you had long ago, and as it was happening, you knew it would forever be burned in your mind, like your graduation day or wedding day; this was one of those moments standing before this massive man-made tribute to modern age. A picture is not worth a thousand words in this case, and a picture does not show the mysterious edifice erected on the Nevada side of the dam. While standing on top of the Hoover Dam and looking toward Nevada, my eyes were immediately drawn to two majestic winged human-like figures cast of bronze standing about 30 feet tall.[189] I like what the sculptor, Oskar J.W. Hansen (1892–1971) called them: The Winged Figures of the Republic. I found myself drawn to them, and

---

[189] The two statues weigh over 4 tons total. For detailed information on this fascinating memorial, goto:
http://www.usbr.gov/lc/hooverdam/History/essays/artwork.html

the closer I got, the more I found myself forced to look upward until I was standing before them with my head cranked straight up, eyes squinting in the light of the Sun and mouth gaping open. Before me, were two mighty human-like angels standing ever-proud with their sharp wings pointing up to the heavens.[190] I studied the figures from tip to toe, and as I was looking down at the pedestal they were on, it was then I noticed with even more amazement what I was standing on. It was not ground but an immense galactic time-chart cut into the polished granite underneath me. Inlaid within it were bronze icons of each planet along the zodiac and many prominent stars. It was obvious, as one of the plaques at the site reveals, that these figures and this star chart are meant to be seen, and like the Hoover Dam, meant to stand the test of time—when all is forgotten, these are meant to be found. As I walked over this cosmological clock to each planet and each star, I noticed that it is all to scale, giving the exact location of each planet relative to the other within our Solar System. I also noticed that the Solar System is in reference to the galactic plane of our galaxy along with other prominent stars like Sirius and Proxima Centauri. This cosmic map reveals the exact location of our planet within our solar system and our solar system within our galaxy at a specific moment in time. The artist believed that whoever, or whatever, stands there, when they measure out the positions of each planet and star inlaid, and then compare them to what they see when they look up into the night sky, will be able to identify the exact moment in time that president Franklin D. Roosevelt dedicated the Hoover Dam: September 30, 1935. You become eerily aware that this timepiece is not meant for us.

---

[190] Ibid.

Time As Metaphor

This astronomical clock is but one of many ways to measure time. Albert Einstein rocked the world and the very foundations of science with his mind-bending proofs revealing that time isn't as granite as we once believed, but in reality, temporal. He developed the math and examples showing time as an actual fourth dimension of space. Just as our three dimensions of height, width, and depth can be shortened or lengthened–so can time. Gone is the assumption that time is untouchable, unchangeable, relentless as captured in so many poems...

> Sonnet 19:
> Devouring Time blunt thou the lion's paws
>
> *Devouring Time blunt thou the lion's paws,*
> *And make the earth devour her own sweet brood,*
> *Pluck the keen teeth from the fierce tiger's jaws,*
> *And burn the long-lived phoenix, in her blood,*
> *Make glad and sorry seasons as thou fleet'st,*
> *And do whate'er thou wilt swift-footed Time*
> *To the wide world and all her fading sweets.*
> *But I forbid thee one most heinous crime:*
> *O, carve not with thy hours my love's fair brow,*
> *Nor draw no lines there with thine antique pen;*
> *Him in thy course untainted do allow,*
> *For beauty's pattern to succeeding men.*
> *Yet, do thy worst old Time: despite thy wrong,*
> *My love shall in my verse ever live young.*
>
> William Shakespeare (1564–1616)

Thanks to poets and scientists alike, we now understand more about time. Regarding the physics of time, Einstein has explained how speed actually changes time. He proved that the faster an object travels the less time effects that object, *i.e. time slows down*. Light from 156,000 stars has traveled 3,000 years to reach us, without aging and without decaying since time stands still at the speed of light. Imagine the possibilities, traveling the universe and not aging. Now think of the fact that our Earth is speeding around our Sun, the Sun is speeding around our galaxy, and the galaxy is speeding through the universe at over thirteen million mph amongst the Virgo Super Cluster of galaxies. All of these speeds effect our experience of time, making our reality of time unique when compared to a planet in another solar system in another galaxy outside of the Virgo Super Cluster. Interestingly enough, it took an Einstein to prove to us what the Bible has revealed all along, that time is not everywhere. It is not eternal. It does no transcend our universe but part of it:

> *First of all, you must understand that in the last days scoffers will come... They will say, "Where is this 'coming' he promised? Ever since our fathers died, everything goes on as it has since the beginning of creation." But they deliberately forget that long ago by God's word the heavens existed and the earth was formed out of water and by water. ...But do not forget this one thing, dear friends: With the Lord a day is like a thousand years, and a thousand years are like a day. The Lord is not slow in keeping his promise, as some understand slowness. (2 Peter 3:3–9)*

Time is also affected by gravity. We have discovered God's physics on how gravity affects both space and time in an effect known as Gravitational Lensing, first theorized by Swiss-American astro-physicist, Fritz Zwicky (1898–1974). The Hubble Space Telescope captured one of the most dramatic images of this effect when aimed at a seemingly empty place in space using its Deep Field imaging. It discovered Abell 2218, an ocean of galaxies far away clustered in the constellation Draco.[191] You can view this image online. When viewing this image, one can readily see how some of the galaxies are smeared, stretched, and arced. After determining this is not due to some sort of glitch with Hubble, astronomers confirmed Gravitational Lensing to be the cause.

The distorted galaxies shown in the image are actually behind the cluster, and as their light waves pass through it they are bent, lengthened, shortened, and curved by the "choppy waters" of gravity in this crowded ocean of galaxies. The very fabric of Space: height, width, and depth, along with the fourth dimension of time, are all severely distorted.

All of us, however, feel like time is relentless, constantly marching on and affected by nothing. Whether you run, walk, or ride a fast motorcycle, time isn't distorted enough to be noticeable. I call this Felt Time.[192] Sir Isaac Newton (1642-1727) was unaware of any other forms of time. He built Classical Physics around this idea of time for all practical purposes, and for their age it worked fine. If illustrated, Felt Time would look like this:

---

[191] Astronomers estimate the distance to be about two billion light years away.
[192] Popular cosmologists and astrophysicists such as Brian Greene refer to this as the Arrow of Time.

Felt Time

When Einstein upset Newton's "applecart" by discovering that time is relative and woven into the very fabric of space, a new idea of time became known to us. This new concept shows time to be bendable, pliable, relative to space and vulnerable to speed and gravity. Such an illustration of time has been drawn by many physicists looking something like a piece of cooked spaghetti:

Relative Time

The Bible also reveals another aspect of time. When Bible scholars review scripture on the idea of time, they see the Bible presenting it both as linear and non-linear. Read these key verses in Scripture and find the repetition among them:

> *He had a dream in which he saw a stairway resting on the earth, with its top reaching to heaven, and the angels of God were ascending and descending on it. There above it stood the LORD, and he said: "I am the LORD, the God of your father Abraham and the God of Isaac. (Genesis 28:12–13)*

> *"This," said the LORD, "is so that they may believe that the LORD, the God of their fathers—the God of Abraham, the God of Isaac and the God of Jacob—has appeared to you." (Exodus 4:3–5)*
>
> *At the time of sacrifice, the prophet Elijah stepped forward and prayed: "O LORD, God of Abraham, Isaac and Israel, let it be known today that you are God..." (1 Kings 18:36–37)*
>
> *But about the resurrection of the dead—have you not read what God said to you, "I am the God of Abraham, the God of Isaac, and the God of Jacob?" He is not the God of the dead but of the living. (Matthew 22:31–33)*
>
> *When Peter saw this, he said to them: '...The God of Abraham, Isaac and Jacob, the God of our fathers, has glorified his servant Jesus." (Acts 3:12–13)*

Did you catch the repetition? *I am the God of Abraham, Isaac, Jacob...* We see the Bible encouraging us to mentally circle back in time before moving forward in time to remember our past, to remember our origins. Sin wants us to forget who we are. God calls us to remember. Thank God that He created memory. If we were an inanimate object, like a bowl, we would only exist in the present time, no memory of the past; we would forget Whose *image and likeness* we were made from and what Jesus Christ did for us. So the Bible reveals time as both mental (past time) and physical (felt time). This circular nature of time is commonly presented by theologians in their seminary classrooms as follows:[193]

Biblical Sense Of Time

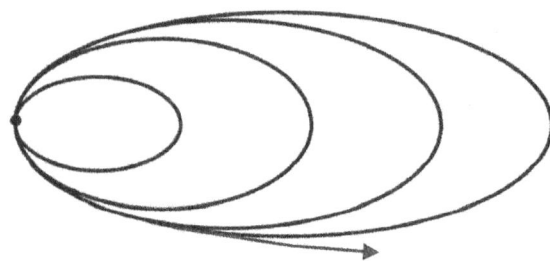

Over the centuries, a few brilliant Church Fathers, such as Irenaeus, Bishop of Lyons (France), further developed the Bible's revelation on time. Irenaeus (130 A.D.–200 A.D. approx.) was a student of the famous theologian Polycarp whom tutored under John, Jesus' beloved disciple. Irenaeus further developed the Bible's Creation account using a non-linear idea of time whereby the Second Adam, Jesus, died on the cross at the exact moment the First Adam fell into sin.[194] How this is done is by treating time as individual events. Each event is then inserted into our space-time like a movie producer splicing scenes into a movie so they appear seamless to us the viewers. An excellent example of time for Irenaeus would be the digital clock. A digital clock causes each second to appear then disappear and a new second to appear. It is disjointed and non-flowing but feels continuous to us because we have the mental capacity to remember past time.[195] Such an illustration would look like this:

---

[193] Grenz, Stanley, D. Guretzki, C.F. Nordling. *Pocket Dictionary of Theological Terms*. InterVarsity Press: Downers Grove, 1999. Print. (p.114)

[194] Known commonly as 'Recapitulation." Steenberg, M.C. *Irenaeus on Creation: The Cosmic Christ and the Saga of Redemption.* BRILL: Boston, 2008. Print.

[195] Ibid.

God Can Treat Time as Individual Events (Digital Time):

ooooooooooooo

We Experience Time as Seamless Events (Felt Time):

St. Augustine (354 A.D.–430 A.D.), our greatest Church Father, championing the foundations of western theology, further developed the Bible's mental facet of time. In his *Confessions, volume 11*, he explains time in Trinitarian language as, "three mental states: past, present, future. For then they could exist at one and the same instant within the mind."[196] This idea works since you and I are aware of the past, present, and future while inanimate objects are only existing in the present. So Time-Past and Time-Future are mental exercises, meta-physical states-of-mind. And like Irenaeus' concept of time, Augustine also explains the Creation events as an "indivisible instant" that appears to us as a seamless timeline in history.[197] St. Augustine, however, along with philosophers through the ages to this present day, confesses that the idea of time is essentially ungraspable. Paraphrasing St. Augustine, he once said: I know what time is, if no one asks me, but not if I have to explain it.[198]

---

[196] Sorabji, Richard. *Time, Creation, and the Continuum*. Cornell University Press: New York, 1983. Print. (p.29)

[197] Reymond, Russell. *A New Systematic Theology of Christian Faith*. Thomas Nelson Publishers: Nashville, 1998. Print. (p.392)

[198] Sorabji, Richard. *Time, Creation, and the Continuum*. Cornell University Press: New York, 1983. Print. (p.29)

So a Christian Spaceview of time embraces duality by recognizing and integrating all these realities of time into a single model of time. It shows our Felt Time is actually made up of Einstein's Relative Time spliced into Irenaeus' Digital Time, but feels seamless to us. Simultaneously, biblical time and St. Augustine's Mental Time work in the non-physical reality of our immaterial conscious mind and soul. And these dual realities of the material and immaterial work together:

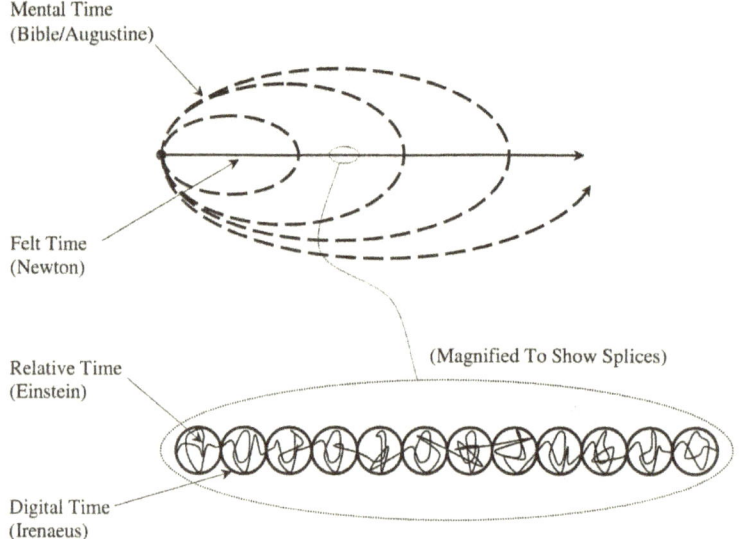

The Christian Spaceview of time with its dual nature strikes a critical blow to today's popular Big Bang theory that relies on a consistent linear idea of time (Newtonian Felt Time). If time was nothing more than Felt Time, then the Big Bang theory's calculations that the cosmos have existed for about 13.7 billion years and human life evolved only over the last 4.5 billion years of our solar system's existence would be an accurate assessment. But, the assumption that time has remained unchanged and linear since the beginning is untenable; time is not linear but only feels to be so. According to this working model (courtesy of NASA.gov), which as you can see uses Felt Time, first was the *Quantum Fluctuation*, then *Inflation* followed by an *Afterglow* caused by intense radiation (light

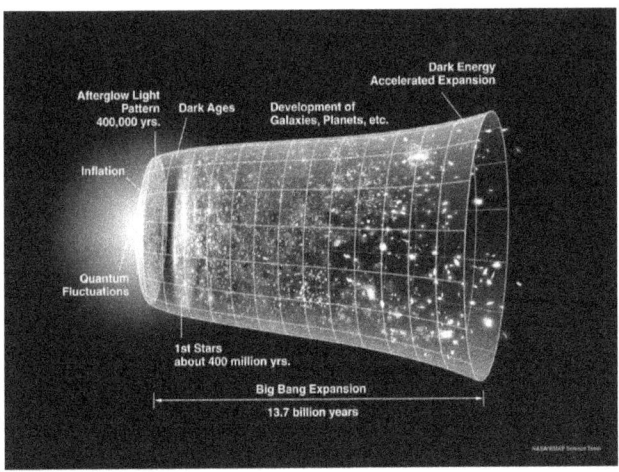

but not as we know it). An era then existed in our young universe where it went dark, utterly. The universe was pitch-black until it cooled enough for atoms to form and photons to exist. It is only at this point, that the laws of our universe as we know it came into existence. Before this moment, cosmologists have sarcastically labeled it the Dark Ages, in which time and space did not exist as we know them today. Even the largest atom-smasher in the world, the LHC, is in jeopardy of pseudo-science as it attempts to understand our origins because of this untenable foundation. Theoretical physicists are trying to model the beginning of time by smashing particles together to view what they believe simulates the Big Bang theory, but they are carrying out the tests within the context of our space-time fabric. The Big Bang occurred outside of our space-time. Their testing is flawed at its most fundamental level. This is where science breaks out of its intended role, the study of the natural, the measurable, the knowable;

stumbling around in the un-natural and perhaps even the super-natural.

Since we now understand how time is not necessarily linear, we can then visualize the six days of Creation found in the book of Genesis to possibly be six individual events (Irenaeus/Einstein/Bible) that the Great Filmmaker then spliced into our timeline at the Quanta level (quantum physics) causing it to look instant and seamless to us (Newtonian/Felt Time) as Six days. Modern theologians refer to this idea of time being spliced and manipulated by God as "Ideal-Time" Theory.[199] We now see how time is not as it seems.

Time Travel

This subject merits a whole book of its own. However, I do want to briefly state two critical aspects that a Christian Spaceview of time recognizes while TV and Hollywood consistently fail to recognize in their respective shows and movies.

Since humans are *imago Dei* beings, we possess a dual nature whereby the immaterial soul is housed in a material body. We discussed this earlier in the book. Since time has been proven to be pliable, it makes time travel theoretically possible. If we develop the technology to loop time back into itself, a person that crosses over at this intersection then theoretically goes back in time—body and soul. And say they were to go back in time and happen to arrive right before their very own conception. Now mind you, they are not there in the same place as the conception but they are on the globe in the same time. Because they are there body and soul, either the baby dies at the point of

---

[199] Erickson, Millard. *Christian Theology*. 2nd ed. 1983. Baker Books: Grand Rapids, 2000. Print. (p.406)

conception or the back-in-time person dies. One or the other—both cannot live. God appoints only one soul to each human being. The Apostle Paul writes, *"Just as people are destined to die once, and after that to face judgment,"(Hebrews 9:27)* So in this odd scenario, you can't help but wonder...which one gets the soul? A Christian Spaceview recognizes that at the point of conception is when a soul is appointed to the newly formed baby. Conception is a miracle and it is holy. Because of this holy event, conception would take priority over the poor time traveler. The time traveler would lose their soul and die instantly.

TV and Hollywood tend to only consider the physical ramifications of time travel, failing to realize that humans are *imago Dei* life–body and soul.

Science Has Answers, Not Necessarily Truth

Immanuel Kant (1724–1804) was an influential philosopher in western history that played a key role in molding how western society thinks of reality (for better or for worse), he foresaw the direction science was heading and explained their treacherous path this way:

> *...genuine scientific knowledge is possible but that this knowledge is of 'phenomenal' reality – that is, reality as it appears to us, rather than reality as it is in itself.*[200]

---

[200] Evans, C. Stephen. *Pocket Dictionary of APOLOGETICS & PHILOSOPHY of RELIGION*. Intervarsity Press: Downers Grove, 2002. Print.

In other words, science is only able to understand and explain that which can be known and measured, and even then science is not meant to find truth, just answers.

An argument can be made that modern science is obsessed with the origin of all things because it has wandered away from its origins. A Christian Spaceview of time is grounded in God's Word and employs science to further enrich humanity's understanding of this realm we now live in. This richer view allows humanity to understand rationally how all things are possible, even six days of Creation as the Word of God reveals. Anyone who discounts Genesis one's Creation account cannot do so from the argument of not enough time. They are simply using time as their mask to hide a deeper reason—a lack of faith in an all-powerful Creator God.

A Christian Spaceview of time recognizes this fatal flaw in cosmologists interpretation of time and on the end of time. The Kepler Mission does not prove such fatalistic notions. Let's see what a Christian Spaceview has to say about the end-times.

11. END-TIMES QUAGMIRE

The heavens will disappear with a roar; the elements will be destroyed by fire, and the earth and everything in it will be laid bare.

—2 Peter 3:11

For if men do these things when the tree is green, what will happen when it is dry? (Luke 23:28–31) This prophecy of the Earth going dry is covered year after year of late in *National Geographic Magazine*. They project fresh water in Asia to be worth more than gold within 50 years. Luke scribed this unsettling prophecy onto papyrus paper while ancient photons were only one-third of their way toward Earth. Luke's gospel, and a good portion of the New Testament, were meticulously copied and sealed in clay jars for safekeeping by the Essenes, a secluded sect of Christianity. It is believed the members of this sect were killed and buildings destroyed during Roman Emperor Nero's siege on Jerusalem in 66 A.D. The locations of these sealed and hidden scrolls died with them. Two thousand years later the clay jars with these scrolls were stumbled upon and these oldest of New Testament texts proved to the world that our current Bible has remained unchanged as it was then. This amazing discovery gives further credence to the reliability of Scripture, which can be extended to the reliability of what prophetic scripture reveals about the end of time. End-time prophecy provides the final argument against intelligent life existing in our sinverse.

Kepler is the tenth mission in NASA's Discovery Class of missions. It is the goal of the Discovery Class of missions to find alien life. As we now see from Kepler's wildly successful planet finding campaign, that it is reasonable to think other Earths (similar gravity, mass, land, water, oxygen, orbital period, etc...) exist. I also believe Kepler's follow-up mission, the James Webb Space Telescope, stands a reasonable chance of identifying signatures of life on Kepler's newfound habitable worlds. However, regarding the search for *intelligent* alien life, we have seen in previous chapters that this is not just a question for the natural sciences. We now see that when it comes to the question on intelligent life, anywhere, theology must be applied first in order to establish where to look for such *imago Dei* life. Modern science has yet to be able to define what intelligent life is, because they are coming at it from the wrong context. Intelligent life is first spiritual in nature and then material in nature. Intelligent life has a dual nature. Therefore, NASA's ultimate quest to discover other intelligent beings will prove to be futile because their foundation is a god-less one when the subject matter is a Godly one. End-Time theology supports this reality as well.

Annihilating Heaven & Earth

Many New York Times bestselling Christian novels play out riveting tales on the end of the world based off the most popular evangelical view of biblical end-time prophecy. This end-time theology was made popular through Lewis Sperry Chafer, founder of Dallas Theological Seminary, and the 1909/1917 editions of the popular Scofield Reference Bible—the Bible I spiritually grew up using and love.[201] It draws its annihilation theology from passages like:

> *Then I saw a new heaven and a new earth, for the first heaven and the first earth had passed away. (Revelation 21:1)*
>
> *The heavens will disappear with a roar; the elements will be destroyed by fire, and the earth and everything in it will be laid bare. ...That day will bring about the destruction of the heavens by fire, and the elements will melt in the heat. But in keeping with his promise we are looking forward to a new heaven and a new earth, the home of righteousness. (2 Peter 3:10b,13)*

2 Peter states, *The heavens*, which is in the plural form, meaning everything…our whole sinverse. But what if, despite my arguments otherwise, you still think other intelligent life is out there in this universe? What will happen to them? Will they all "burn" too? You have run into a theological quagmire of the "third kind."[202] Here is why:

The Bible states, *"He is the Rock, his works are perfect, and all his ways are **just**. A faithful God who does no wrong, upright and **just** is he (Deuteronomy 32:4) [bold mine].* God is Just. It would be unjust for God to annihilate an entire race of intelligent alien beings in our universe when judgment falls upon our universe in the end-time. Our sin is not there sin. Therefore, one cannot both believe God is going to annihilate "heaven and earth," which means our universe, and also believe that intelligent aliens exist in this

---

[201] Reymond, Russell. *A New Systematic Theology of Christian Faith*. Thomas Nelson Publishers: Nashville, 1998. Print. (p.985)
[202] From the blockbuster 1977 movie: *Close Encounters of the Third Kind* by Steven Spielberg.

same universe. Because of this dilemma, one must choose from three hard choices:

1. God is not a Just God.
2. The Bible is wrong in declaring the annihilation of all things.
3. Alien *imago Dei* do not exist in our universe.

Now before lightning strikes me, let me quickly state that God is indeed a Just God as ancient Scripture and Christian doctrine profess. So the choices quickly narrow to two. Again, the choice is clear since the Bible is never wrong (just misunderstood). This leaves us with choice #3) Alien i*mago Dei* cannot exist in our universe.

However, some may still think these choices are way too simplified and insist that other intelligent life must exist here due to the sheer size of it all. It is tempting. Especially when you consider a hundred billion plus galaxies adding up to over four hundred trillion stars total…this makes a tempting case for cold, hard math. But there are two fundamental flaws with this temptation: First, such a position indicates a prejudice toward science over God's Word, which is no wonder since our culture is completely immersed in such positivistic thought. The second flaw is placing the material realm over the immaterial realm. Science studies the material realm; theology studies the immaterial realm. By leaning more on cold, hard math; it reveals a failure to acknowledge the relevance of God's Word on the dual nature of intelligent life. Since intelligent beings are *imago Dei* beings, theology plays the foundational role in the discussion of other intelligent life in which modern science must then launch from. Duality exists in the discussion of intelligent life but modern science ignores this. Do not be fooled by their false interpretations based on Kepler's discoveries of so many habitable worlds.

Redeeming Heaven & Earth

However, regarding choice #2…about the "Bible being wrong in declaring the annihilation of all things." There is a revision taking place to popular end-time theology happening in seminaries around the country as we speak.[203] This revision began to develop through much discourse among biblical scholars and was pioneered by Dutch theologian, Abraham Kuyper (1837–1920). This revision champions the idea of a redeeming God over a destructive God. *i.e. grace over judgment.* Instead of completely annihilating our universe, God completely *refines* it. Here is one of the key biblical texts:

> *For no one can lay any foundation other than the one already laid, which is Jesus Christ. If any man builds on this foundation using gold, silver, costly stones, wood, hay or straw, his work will be shown for what it is, because the Day will bring it to light. It will be revealed with fire, and the fire will test the quality of each man's work. If what he has built survives, he will receive his reward. If it is burned up, he will suffer loss; he himself will be saved, but only as one escaping through the flames.*
> *(1 Corinthians 3:10b-15)*

---

[203] George Eldon Ladd of the Dispensational Camp titles it the "Moderate Futurist View" in his book, *A Theology of the New Testament*, p.682.

Although the context of this passage is on salvation today, it does have significant theological implications that can be applied to end-time theology. The key implication being that a person's good works survives the *"fire."* Theologians like Kuyper take this passage to mean that God will not annihilate but actually keep the good things and burn the rest. We could go on about this, but I want to jump ahead to an intriguing question...where is God going to put all this good stuff? It would make sense that God would keep them on Earth, this same Earth but with evil purged from it, refined by fire, so it is all made new again and ready to be re-assimilated back into God's *good* Creation. This developing understanding is indeed more consistent with accounts in Scripture where God chooses to spare mankind, as in the account of Noah's ark in the Old Testament and our Lord and Savior Jesus Christ dying on the cross on our behalf in the New Testament. Many scholarly papers and books are now available on this grace-emphasized interpretation of end-time theology in Christian bookstores across the country today.[204]

End-Time Duality

This refinement to end-time theology does not change the three choices I originally presented but does dig deeper into the second choice. It highlights how annihilation carries with it a dual function of annihilation and redemption (duality). God has the sovereign right to annihilate and the sovereign right to redeem. This provides further understanding into Paul's declaration in Ephesians,

---

[204] Wittmer, Michael. *Heaven is a Place on Earth*. Zondervan: Grand Rapids, 2004. Print. An excellent book on this subject. This shift in end-time thinking does not mean all people will ultimately go to heaven, hell is real and unfortunately will be packed forever.

> *And he made known to us the mystery of his will according to his good pleasure, which he purposed in Christ, to be put into effect when the times will have reached their fulfillment—to bring **all things together** under Christ. (Ephesians 1:10)[bold mine]*

By God executing justice against our moral sin and annihilation of our universe's physical entropy, He will make us and our universe capable to merge back with Him once again in His *good* Creation. As the text indicates, God is bringing *all things together* once again. So by annihilating, God is also redeeming. I like how Millard J. Erickson concludes his understanding of the new Heaven and new Earth in his systematic theology work, *Christian Theology*:

> *As we carry out our role, however, we must also be mindful that eschatology pertains primarily to a **new realm** beyond space and time, a new heaven and a new earth.*[205]*[bold mine]*

Like Erickson's theory of a *"new realm"*, String Theory also promotes the existence of other realms beyond ours. Parallel universes could be those realms. Our parallel universe, though, is not a perfect copy but a flawed one where galaxies collide, wars erupt, and children starve to death while billions of dollars are wasted in the search for other intelligent life. Our sinverse, if left untouched by the redeeming hand of God, will surely die. But God will redeem what is His. In the *twinkling of an eye*, that which

---

[205] Erickson, Millard. *Christian Theology*. 2nd Ed. 1983. Baker Books: Grand Rapids, 2000. Print. (p.1170)

he refines will find themselves back in God's presence in His *good* creation:

> *Listen, I tell you a mystery: We will not all sleep, but we will all be changed- in a flash, in the twinkling of an eye, at the last trumpet. (1 Corinthians 15:51–52)*

And when God purges sin and entropy from our corrupted reality, making all things new again, the redeemed in Christ will once again be able to gaze up at those familiar constellations. But this time the perplexing questions will not arise within us like the days of old. This time, the stars will not tease us. Instead, we will find the heavens as God intended them to be—a never-ending playground beckoning all His redeemed *imago Dei* to explore and enjoy forevermore.

12. WE'VE LISTENED...WATCHED...BUT HAVE WE LEARNED?

> *...the universe itself has no single history, nor even an independent existence. ...but every possible history.*
>
> ~Richard Feynman
> (1918–1988)
> Physicist/Atheist

The coffee has long since gone cold and the night's dew is heavy upon my telescope. I rub my eyes, stretch, and begin dismantling my scope from my father's equatorial mount. It's been a good night of viewing, discovering, and thinking. While tearing down the scope and mount, I find myself whispering, *Thank you, God, for this space, this time.* For even in this world filled with such misery and chaos, it's moments like these—amongst a chorus of crickets under a canopy of countless stars—that I am reminded of what we used to have so long ago…and will have again someday.

Take It Back

The study of the heavens helps us understand our place in this natural order: no longer do we pride ourselves with a center of the universe conceit but a much humbler position and have astronomy to thank for this. Astronomy continues to humble and inspire those who dare to learn from it and NASA's Kepler Mission is no exception. This successful mission ended in 2013 leaving us with thousands of planet candidates for Kepler's science team and their host of ground-based telescopes to scrutinize. It has changed our age-old mindset on the stars we see at night. The hunt is on and all eyes in the astronomical community and major news outlets around the world are watching the continued results from this historic mission. Such success has proven that planet formation is a natural function across our universe. A universe the 2MASS Sky Survey shows to hold over a hundred billion galaxies each harboring hundreds of billions of stars—and this just in our seeable universe. Such grandeur all around us forces profound thoughts on deep things, things like our significance, alien life, alien intelligent life, and if they would know Jesus.

Men with a heritage of Christian faith like Copernicus, Galileo, Kepler, Brahe, and Newton pioneered modern science only for it to be given over to scientists outspoken in their god-less worldviews. It isn't the data they discover that I question, but the interpretations of the data that must be questioned. Recognizing this important difference requires Christians to apply critical thinking skills.[206] Thinking critically helps us discern fact from interpretation, like the first page of that big picture book I read to my children.

To be motivated to develop such critical skills, remember these five Christian Spaceview truths:

First Truth: Conflict is okay; it should be embraced and not avoided. Many people find themselves embroiled

---

[206] This is no longer taught in public education due to a liberal shift toward positivistic education models in the latter half of the 19th century. American schools for almost two hundred years developed children's critical thinking skills via a liberal arts education system. Private schools and colleges are also now falling away from this uniquely American approach in order to comply to federal standards. With the loss of critical thinking skills comes the loss of innovation.

in a silent conflict between science and faith. Do not frame it as an ultimatum.

Second Truth: The strength of your faith is not built on piety. Piety is well illustrated in the Bible by the religious leaders of Jesus day—the ones he yelled at.

Third Truth: an unshakeable Christian faith is built on reason. Use these five tools to keep God's Word in its proper context: Grammar, Genre, Historicity, Context and Exposition.

Fourth Truth: Blind faith does not exist. A person must first become aware in something or in someone before they can choose to believe or not believe. So faith, in anything, first requires information.

Fifth and Final Truth: Recognize the difference between the scientific discovery and how scientists *interpret* the scientific discovery. Kepler's discovery of other habitable worlds like Earth is only a matter of time and this should not be where the conflict is as a Christian. Instead, the conflict should be in the *interpretation* presented by god-less scientists and the mainstream media.

These five truths will help maintain the guiding principle in a Christian Spaceview: *Do not let scientists tell you **what** to believe in but how to better understand **Who** you believe in.*

Christians thinking critically will prove a must with NASA's exciting news. Charles Malik, former U.S. Ambassador to Lebanon, United Nations General Assembly President, and three-time president of the U.N. Security Council, had this to say during his inaugural address at the Billy Graham Center for Wheaton College:

> *Therefore if evangelization is the most important task, the task that comes immediately after it...is not politics, or economics...I must be frank with you: The greatest danger besetting American evangelical Christianity is the danger of anti-intellectualism. The mind...is not cared for enough...evangelicals cannot afford to keep on living on the periphery of responsible intellectual existence.*[207]

A lack of critical thinking hinders the Christian community's ability to reach and impact our science-idolizing western culture. Having this ability to recognize truth from bias will not only shore up one's own faith, but instill a quiet confidence to engage the conversations around us when the headlines hit: "OTHER EARTHS FOUND!" Sharp-dressed talking-heads clamoring away on all major news media outlets will, as usual, host scientists presenting god-less interpretations of such history making discoveries emanating from the Northern Cross. We can be that witness, standing in the wilderness of skeptics, presenting a clear pro-science/pro-Bible response. *I.e. Duality.* Choosing to not be this voice of reason will prove a missed opportunity for the lost and confused who are looking for meaning in this life and something to believe in. Be that witness of truth during these exciting days of planet hunting.

Just as we have looked at famous scientists, we have also looked at Classical Physics, Relativity Physics and Quantum Physics—only to start wondering where this winding road of modern science is taking us. Is it driving us closer to our Creator, illuminating our minds with truth; or

---

[207] Malik, Charles, *The Two Tasks*. Cornerstone Books: Metairie, 1980. Print. (p.33)

is it taking us down another road, a darker fatalistic road. As we have seen, cosmology and biology have made a few wrong turns. Biology has reduced humans to mere animals. Cosmologists have reduced the universe, so delicately balanced for life, into nothing more than a chaos-driven wind-up toy with no purpose. At the same time, these same disciplines now recognize concepts that were once hailed as nonsense when theologians presented them ages ago. Concepts like duality, which the brilliant minds of our Christian forefathers established when they declared Jesus Christ to be 100% God–100% man. Other realms like Heaven and Hell, which mathematical proofs show the need for ten total dimensions in String Theory. So String Theory inadvertently gives the biblical idea of Heaven and Hell legitimacy in the halls of science. And finally, science now recognizes how the impossible is possible with Heisenberg's Uncertainty Principle. This principle explains quantum tunneling, which explains how radiation can exist and even how Jesus walked through a closed door. No longer can scientists and their science diminish concepts revealed in the ancient texts of the Bible as myth and fairy tales just because they seem outlandish or impossible. All things are possible with God, as physics and physicists are just beginning to realize.

    We also learned how spacecrafts like COBE and WMAP have shown how ninety-five percent of the matter and energy needed to hold a galaxy together is unseen, unknown, unmeasured. This is crushing news for Atheists and Agnostics. They must realize that they are basing their everlasting existence and peace of mind on a paltry 5% knowledge base. This is not enough evidence to make such a profound life decision. If that isn't disconcerting enough, this 5% knowledge base is also known to be flawed as one physics professor and atheist honestly confides:

> *We take quarks, black holes, and the big bang story to be objective elements...of an external, independent reality. We forget or suppress the fact that all of these elements are ideas that came originally from the human mind, as do all the arguments we use to justify them...science is the product of human imagination, thought, insight, and genius...The whole structure and content of science...is like a vast and intricate game whose rules, playing board, and pieces were all created by human beings for their own use, benefit, amusement, power, and security.*[208]

Science is a metaphor for a god-less reality. Even Hawking confesses that scientists can fudge their proofs to prove what they want, and that this is, *...not an uncommon occurrence in science.*[209] A good example of this was NASA's Stardust Mission. This probe successfully weaved in and out of comet Wild 2 capturing glycine, a vital protein required in all carbon-based life, moving many scientists to interpret the data as further evolutionary proof that the seeds of life on Earth came from comets. But their linear timeline requires billions of years of cosmic evolution. A creationist, however, can take this same discovery to argue a young universe by showing that the building blocks of life were present in the very beginning. Each camp interprets the data to fit their worldview. Duality, however, would argue they are both correct, since time is relative and vulnerable to manipulation...capable of looking ancient and instant simultaneously. Many god-less

---

[208] Jones, Roger S. *Physics for the Rest of Us.* Contemporary Books: Chicago, 1992. Print. (p.133)
[209] Hawking, Stephen. *A Brief History of Time.* A Bantam Book: New York, 1996. Print. (p.44)

people then cry foul complaining that God would not lie and trick us with such movie-maker special effects.[210] I find this argument suspect since these are the same people who dismiss theology yet quick to grab it when they believe it serves their god-less agendas. As much as they do not like to hear it, the human mind cannot fathom all things, it cannot understand the ways of God. Furthermore, God is not obligated to explain His ways and physics to us. But of course, this response has proven unacceptable for scientists and thus they forge ahead pioneering their own grand story. Hawking explains how scientific pursuits are not about truth but about creating models to interpret reality in ways that make sense for the moment and must change as needed.[211] Hawking even goes so far as to say the ancient Ptolemaic model of the celestial movements (that Brahe was defending) were as legitimate as Copernicus' heliocentric model (which Kepler was defending). Two scientists with a Christian worldview observe it this way:

> *...studies in the history and sociology of science seemed to strengthen the suspicion that the conclusions of science were less direct product of objective scientific inquiry than the product of largely unseen subjective and social forces...*[212]

The sciences, especially Cosmology, have shown to be metaphorical, subjective to the times and fads of the day. Scientists confess to construct their own interpretation of reality that many others in the scientific community then rush to support.

---

[210] Hawking, Stephen. *The Grand Design*. A Bantam Book: New York, 2010. Print.
[211] Ibid. (p.6)
[212] Chappell, Dorothy, David E. Cook. *Not Just Science.* Zondervan: Grand Rapids, 2005. Print. (p.54)

In contrast to this ghetto the god-less are driving through, the biblical concept has remained unchanged, no matter the era or empire. The Bible has always revealed that we are not alone. We've learned how God is with us. We've also learned how evil is with us. Make no mistake, we are not alone. Scripture also reveals that the Triune God interacts within our space-time sinverse. God desires His Creation to know Him and goes to great lengths to draw His *imago Dei* (image of God) back into a fulfilling relationship with Him.

Not only does our Triune God desire to walk with us but the second-person of the Trinity, the Son of God, provides the way. And not just for humans, but for all God's *imago Dei* life no matter where or when they exist. If alien *imago Dei* life exist and have rebelled against God, their rebellion, like ours, perverts their physical reality uniquely, phasing them out of God's *good* Creation into a perverted parallel universe slightly out of phase with God's *good* Creation. As astrophysicists see in the ramifications of String Theory and M-theory, multiple universes (multiverse) may exist and as theologians agree, it is certainly within the capability of an eternal God to create them. An eternal God is not confined to the laws of our universe nor any others. Those struggling with an anemic faith may find such spectacular thoughts deeply unsettling, an assault to their tidy idea of God. Such concepts are radical departures from traditional Christian thinking since they are not mentioned in the Bible. The Bible's context is an earthly one, concerned exclusively with earthlings. It also provides glimpses into the eternal. The Bible was written within our context of space-time. God inspired a personal book for you and me because He is a personal God. He is our Creator. God hears *our* cries and has shown *us* The Way in His marvelous Word. And although alien intelligent life would not know our Jesus from

Nazareth, they indeed know the Son of God. For our eternal triune God is a Just God. Karl Barth argued, that the Son of God is a Cosmic Redeemer.[213]

And our Triune God is Just. It would be unjust for God to force alien *imago Dei* to be annihilated during our end-time saga. To understand the concept why alien *imago Dei* cannot exist in our sinverse, we first must take the catastrophic consequences of the Fall in Genesis chapter three seriously. These consequences are seen two-fold: The Fall is seeable and measurable in nature and called entropy. And, the Fall is knowable meta-physically and called sin. Having established this fuller understanding of the Fall, we must then come to understand the proper understanding of life. Theologians have established a deeper, fuller understanding of life with many books written on what intelligent life is throughout the centuries. To help define life, scholars studying the book of Genesis recognize three basic categories: Lower Life Forms, Higher Life Forms, and Intelligent Life Forms. Intelligent life forms are a quantum leap beyond the lower and higher forms of life. Using this definition of life, we then considered the question of alien life. Exobiologists may very well find signatures of lower life using the future James Webb Space Telescope, since such life can be pursued with cold, hard math—where one plus one equals two. Higher life forms, however, are more than mere physical beings. Scripture reveals how they have been granted God's *breath of life*, one plus one no longer equals two. The natural just merged with the super-natural.

And then we must descend further in and deeper down, where reverence and awe are required as we enter the midst of the sacred and mysterious: Intelligent life.

---

[213] Church Dogmatiks

Intelligent conscious beings must transcend all other categories of life since such life exists in two realms at once, the material (ontic/physical) construct of our body and the immaterial (moral/spiritual) essence intertwined within it giving us our consciousness. This consciousness emanates from a holy image—*imago Dei*. Such sacred beings should not be categorized in the Animal Kingdom alongside rats as biologists have done. *Imago Dei* life demands a category all their own: *Kingdom—imago Dei*. Such sacred beings also possess a holy purpose: seeking harmony with God, others, self, and the planet in order to properly reflect God's *image and likeness*.

On a brief side note, such a kingdom recognition would never allow the current pop-culture phenomenon we now see in museums: de-skinned dead humans propped up in poses for the ticket-paying masses to look at. *Imago Dei* beings are more than mere animals but fused with a sacred essence that requires our reverence. When humans die, the tissue and bones symbolize the temple that once housed a transcendent and holy presence. Viewing the dead is irreverent, dark and symbolic of what modern science thinks of human life…what it thinks of me and you: Meaningless. Entertainment.

Alien *imago Dei* would also be with God and very possibly in the same original *good* Creation God created us in as revealed in Genesis one and two. But, if they rebel and fall away from God, they are then separated from God and His *good* Creation into a corrupted copy all their own. This is why neither NASA nor any other human organization will be able to find alien intelligent life in our universe. Our universe is our sinverse.

And not only have we looked at space but also at time, the fourth dimension. Such great scholars as Irenaeus,

Einstein, and St. Augustine reveal how time is far more elusive and complex than what we see and feel. Cosmologists talk about the first few seconds of the theoretical Big Bang and how the universe is 13.7 billion years old based on an untenable Newtonian idea that time is unchanging, linear, and untouchable. But as scientists, philosophers, and theologians have shown; it is a mistake to use time as the key metric on such discussions. Einstein revealed to the world how Time is a dimension that stretches, compresses, bends and loops along with Space. The force that can manipulate and warp Time is Gravity. Higgs boson is the elusive particle that is believed to cause gravity in all things. The LHC has identified this particle and when science learns how to harness it, they can then harness the power of Time. The Great Filmmaker reserves all copyrights on Time and can splice it without need for explanation. But we don't see time for what it truly is but only how it feels to us—unrelenting.

And finally, we must look at end-time theology. It provides the final argument for why intelligent alien life cannot exist in our sinverse since God is a Just God. The Bible reveals the annihilation of Heaven and Earth at the end of our time. If other intelligent life exists, this would mean the genocide of these beings due to human sin, which would be unjust. Because of this, anyone who still holds out that other intelligent life may exist in our seeable universe due to the sheer size of it all, is in a theological quagmire of the "third kind." They are faced to choose between three choices: God is not Just; The Bible is wrong in declaring the annihilation of all things; or Alien *imago Dei* do not exist in our universe. Since God is Just and the Bible is not wrong, we are left with the last choice as the only viable option for those who take the Bible and theology seriously.

However, regarding the second choice, the Bible is not wrong but maybe the popular interpretation of end-time theology is. Kuyper provides a much needed refinement here that more reflects the grace found richly in the New Testament. Even so, alien *imago Dei* still cannot exist in our sinverse since our rebellion is not theirs. What this means for NASA's Discovery Class of Missions to find other intelligent life, is that all our money and all there time is in vain. They are looking for intelligent alien life in the wrong place. And NASA does not have the technology to peer into other universes, nor would God allow it. The judgment on the construction of the Tower of Babel is a good example.

All around the world young lovers gaze upon an ocean of stars each night, mesmerized by their beauty and captivated by their mystery. It is in these moments they might dare reveal to each other profound thoughts...*Why do we exist? Why is Space so vast? Is there a God that made it all? What could be out there and will we ever know*? Sadly, these beautiful stars now only serve to remind them and us of what we could have had. God created us as His image-bearers—to be an everlasting people in a never-ending universe. God's *good* Creation was for our discovery and enjoyment forever. We could have had it all...but wanted more. We gave it all up for this. Our broken carbon-copy sinverse is doomed to a slow expanding oblivion if left alone. But God will rescue our broken realm. He promises to redeem all that calls on His Son, Jesus Christ. God's Word confirms that those who believe in the Son of God will be redeemed back into God's *good* creation. And it is there, in God's *good* creation, where our Heavenly Father has created, is creating and will continue to create all sorts of wonderful life for all eternity.

EPILOGUE

Angel Of Light

One final thought...

As impressive as science and technology are, those who trust in it alone, lose at the end. Just read the book of Revelation. Scripture is clear that the future is filled with human suffering on a horrific scale. And Jesus offers disturbing insights into these last days that make me shudder...

> *At that time if anyone says to you, "Look, here is the Christ" or, "There he is" do not believe it. For false Christ's and false prophets will appear and perform great signs and miracles to deceive even the elect—if that were possible. (Matthew 23:23–24)*

I.D.E. Thomas presents a fascinating scenario in his book by Hearthstone Publishing, *Omega Conspiracy.*[214] The author poses the idea that the final battle will begin with Satan and his thugs posing as intelligent alien beings making first contact with us. Hollywood is setting the stage perfectly with blockbuster sci-fi movies (and movies I enjoy). Add to that how astronomers are now discovering whole other worlds and how NASA and SETI[215] both have missions searching for extra-terrestrial life. It would seem that contact with "intelligent aliens" would indeed be the perfect ploy to fool the masses into following the angel of

---

[214] 1997, re-published in 2007
[215] The Search for Extraterrestrial Intelligence (SETI), has been underway for over two decades with no results.

darkness. Who is to say that the Father of Lies would not come up with such a perfect scheme. A Christian Spaceview argues that no other intelligent life exists in our sinverse. So then, the only visitor from outer space could be none other than evil personified—Lucifer and his thugs. As scripture reveals, the Devil can use Scripture to fool us and can reveal himself as light:

And no wonder, for Satan himself masquerades as an angel of light. (2 Corinthians 11:14).

It makes one ponder just what kind of light has been traveling to us these past three thousand years...

References

- Agutter, Paul S., Denys N. Wheatley. *Life Concepts in Modern Biology.* Springer: Netherlands, 2007. Print. (p.118)
- *Atlas Of The Skies.* TAJ Books: Codham, UK, 2003. Print.(p.196)
- Bartusiak, Marcia. *The Day We Found The Universe.* Pantheon Books: New York, 2009. Print. (p. X)
- Ben-Naim, Arieh. *Entropy Demystified.* World Scientific: Hackensack, 2008. Print.
- Bertrand, Russell. *Mysticism and Logic.* New York: Norton, 1929. Print. (pp47-48, 56-57)
- Boyle, Alan. "Millions of Earths? Talk causes a stir." 26 July 2010. Web. <http://cosmiclog.msnbc.msn.com/_news/2010/07/26/4756559-millions-of-earths-talk-causes-a-stir>
- Brunner, Emil. *Man in Revolt: A Christian Anthropology.* 1957. The Lutterworth Press: Cambridge, 2002. Reprint
- Chappell, Dorothy, David E. Cook. *Not Just Science.* Zondervan: Grand Rapids, 2005. Print. (p.44)
- Couper, Heather, N. Henbest. *Endless Universe.* Covent Garden Books: New York, 1999. Print.
- Dunn, James. *Ramesses XI: The Last New Kingdom Pharaoh.* n.d. Web. 26 Mar. 2010. <http://touregypt.net/featurestories/ramessesxi.htm>
- Elwell, Walter A. Editor. "Evangelical Dictionary of Biblical Theology." Baker Books, Grand Rapids: 1996. Print.
- Ericson, Millard. *Christian Theology.* 2nd Ed. 1983. Baker Books: Grand Rapids, 2000. Print.
- Eusebius, *The History of the Church from Christ to Constantine.* Trans. G.A. Williamson. Dorset Press, NY: 1965. Print.
- Evans, C. Stephen. *Pocket Dictionary of APOLOGETICS & PHILOSOPHY of RELIGION.* Intervarsity Press: Downers Grove, 2002. Print.
- Ferris, Timothy. "Worlds Apart." National Geographic Magazine, December 2009. Print. (p.91)
- Fischer S.R. *A History of Writing.* Reaktion Books: London, 2001. Print. (p.90); Hoffman J.M. *In The*

- *Beginning: A Short History of the Hebrew Language*. New York University Press: New York, 2004. Print. (p.3)
- Frankenberry, Nancy. *The Faith of Scientists In Their Own Words*. Princeton University Press: Princeton, 2008. Print.
- George Eldon Ladd, of the Dispensational Camp, titles it the "Moderate Futurist View" in his book, *A Theology of the New Testament*, p.682.
- Goldstein, M., I. Goldstein. *The Refrigerator and the Universe, Understanding the Laws of Energy*. Harvard University Press: London, 2003. Print. (p.387-388)
- Greene, Brian. *The Elegant Universe*. Vintage Books: New York, 2000. Print. (p.97)
- Grenz, Stanley, D. Guretzki, C.F. Nordling. *Pocket Dictionary of Theological Terms*. InterVarsity Press: Downers Grove, 1999. Print. (p.114).
- Hawking, Stephen & Mlodinow L. *The Grand Design*. Bantam Books: New York, 2010. Print. (p.124)
- Hawking, Stephen edited and commentary, *On The Shoulders Of Giants*. Running Press: Philadelphia, 2002. Print.
- Hawking, Stephen. *A Brief History of Time, 10th Anniversary Edition*. A Bantam Book: New York, 2006. Print. (p.57)
- Hawking, Stephen. *A Brief History of Time*. A Bantam Book: New York, 1996. Print.
- Hawking, Stephen. *Universe in a Nutshell.* A Bantam Book: New York, 2001. Print. (p.176)
- Hearnshaw, J.B. *The Analysis of Starlight: One Hundred and Fifty Years of Astronomical Spectroscopy*. Cambridge University Press Syndicate: New York, 1986. Print (p.20)
- Henderson, Mark. "Discovery by Stardust probe in Wild 2 coma suggest life on Earth began in space." *Times Online.* Web. 19 Aug. 2009. < http://www.timesonline.com>
- Jayawardhana, Ray. "Are Super-Sized Earths The New Frontier?" Astronomy, November 2008 (Volume 36, Issue 11). Print.

- Jones, Roger S. *Physics For The Rest Of Us.* Contemporary Books: Chicago, 1992. Print. (p.128)
- Kaku, Michio. *Parallel Worlds.* Doubleday: New York, 2005. Print. (p.160)
- Krauss, Russell. "Vatican Hosts Conference on Alien Life." Boise Liberal Examiner 15 Nov. 2009, Web. 15 Nov. 2009. <http://www.examiner.com/x-6186-Boise-Liberal-Examiner~y2009m11d15-Vatican-hosts-conference-on-alien-worlds-alien-life.html>
- Liddle, Andrew, Jon Loveday. *The Oxford Companion to Cosmology.* Oxford University Press: Oxford, 2008. Print. (p.203)
- Magli, Giulio. *Mysteries And Discoveries of Archaeoastronomy.* Praxis Publishing: New York, 2009. Print.
- Malik, Charles, *The Two Tasks.* Cornerstone Books: Metairie, 1980. Print. (p.33)
- Man, John. *The Terra Cotta Army.* Da Capo Press, 2008. Print.
- Muller, Ingo, Weiss, Wolf. *Entropy and Energy: A Universal Competition.* Springer-Verlaag: Berlin, 2005. Print. (p.233)
- Narr. Pamela Rutherford. *World Today.* BBC on Nat'l Public Radio WUOM, Ann Arbor, Michigan. 11 Sept. 2010. Radio.
- Plantinga, Alvin. *Reason and Belief in God.* University of Notre Dame Press: Notre Dame, 1983. Print. (p.17-18)
- Plantinga, Alvin. *Religion and Science.* 20 Feb. 2007 Web. <http://www.plato.cstanford.edu>
- Poundstone, William. *Carl Sagan: A Life In The Cosmos.* Holt Paperbacks: New York, 2000. Print.
- Powell, Corey. "Unlikely Places." *Scientific American 266*, March 1992: 22. Print.
- Reymond, Russell. *A New Systematic Theology of Christian Faith.* Thomas Nelson Publishers: Nashville, 1998. Print. (p.416)
- Robinson, Keith. *Spectroscopy: The Key to the Stars.* Springer-Verlag: London, 2007. Print. (p.1)
- Russell, Robert J., Nancy Murphy, C.J. Isham. *Quantum Cosmology and the Laws of Nature: Scientific Perspectives on Divine Action.* 2nd Ed.

- Vatican Observatory Publications: Vatican City State; The Center for Theology and the Natural Sciences: Berkeley. 1996. Print.
- Smail, T. *Like Father Like Son.* William B. Eerdmans Publishing: Grand Rapids, 2006. Print. (p.75). As quoted from St. Augustine's fifteen volume work, *De Trinitate,* written between 400 – 416 AD.
- Sorabji, Richard. *Time, Creation, and the Continuum.* Cornell University Press: New York, 1983. Print. (p.29)
- Steenberg, M.C.. *Irenaeus on Creation: The Cosmic Christ and the Saga of Redemption.* BRILL: Boston, 2008. Print.
- Vergano, Dan. "Kepler's on a mission to discover 'Earth's.'" *USA TODAY* 5 Mar. 2009, Section 6D. Print.
- Voelkel, James. *Johannes Kepler and the New Astronomy.* Oxford University Press: Cary, 1999. Print.
- Wittmer, Michael. *Heaven is a Place on Earth.* Zondervan: Grand Rapids, 2004. Print. (p.21)
- "*NASA Finds Direct Proof of Dark Matter.*" Release 06-297. Web. 21 Aug. 2006. <http://www.NASA.gov./news.html>
- "The Search for Extraterrestrial Life." Narr. Diane Rehm. *The Diane Rehm Show*. Natl. Public Radio. WAMU, Washington, 20 Aug. 2009. Radio. Kepler Science Team attendees: Jill Tarter, Jon Jenkins, Alan Boss.